SAN JUAN ICE CLIMBS

A GUIDE TO SELECT ICE CLIMBS IN THE SAN JUAN MOUNTAINS

Damon Johnston

Mountain World Media LLC
Telluride, Colorado

For more information on books published by Mountain World Media LLC. please visit
www.mountainworldmedia.com or send an email to damon@mountainworldmedia.com

Distributed by
AlpenBooks, 4602 Chennault Beach Rd., Ste B1, Mukilteo WA 98275
800-290-9898 / cserve@alpenbooks.com
and
Bookswest, 11111 E 53rd Ave, Ste A, Denver, CO 80239
303-449-5995 / 800-378-4188 / www.bookswest.com.

First Edition: Unknown
Second Edition: 1996
Third Edition: 2009

ISBN 978-0-9763309-4-3

Cover photograph by Charlie Fowler / Climber: Ben Clark in the Ouray Ice Park

Printed in China

TABLE OF CONTENTS

IN MEMORY OF CHARLIE FOWLER

AUTHOR'S NOTE

Welcome to the long-needed update to Charlie Fowler's handwritten (and out of print) "San Juan Ice Climbs." Although I have not added many new routes, there are several additions to specific areas such as the Ouray Ice Park and Telluride. Keeping things to a bare minimum—not too many photos or long route descriptions—this guidebook is designed to get you to the base of a select group of classic ice climbs in the San Juan Mountains. I will continue to seek out information to areas which are not covered in great detail such as Lake City and Wolf Creek Pass and will post all updates to: www.sanjuaniceclimbs.com.

It's important to emphasize that this is a guide to **select** "water ice" climbs and does not include every route you may have heard about around the campfire or at the bar. That said, if you are aware of additional routes not covered in this guide and think they should be represented in future editions, please send new route information (location, name, grade, FA, photo, etc) to: damon@mountainworldmedia.com.

Mixed routes of the San Juans will be covered in much greater detail in Volume 2, slated for a winter 2010 release. If you have any knowledge of mixed routes for this region of Colorado, please email the location, name, grade, FA, etc. to: damon@mountainworldmedia.com. All informational sources will be acknowledged appropriately.

FIRST ASCENTS (FAs)

This topic could take several pages to debate so FA information has been excluded. In the end, it is often hard to say when a route was first climbed and by whom.

THE GOLDEN RULES

Bring an extra hat, an extra pair of gloves, a headlamp, and an insulated jacket with you on EVERY adventure. Check to make sure batteries are in working condition before you depart and change your picks as needed (they can become fatigued and fail). Stay hydrated!

The Access Fund keeps climbing areas open and conserves the climbing environment.

The Access Fund supports and represents over 1.6 million climbers nationwide in ALL forms of climbing: rock climbing, ice climbing, mountaineering, and bouldering. Five core programs support the mission on national and local levels: public policy, stewardship and conservation (including grants), grassroots activism, climber education, and land acquisition. Become a member today!

AREA MAP

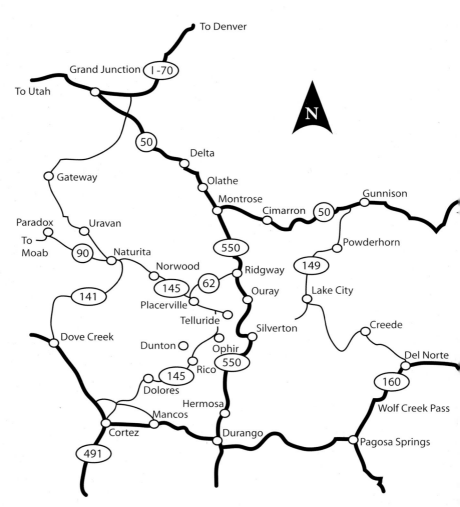

Times From Cities & Towns To Ouray	
(Hours : Minutes)	
Denver	6:10
Grand Junction	2:10
Durango	1:30
Pagosa Springs	2:50
Cortez	2:40
Gunnison	2:00
Telluride	1:10
Moab UT	3:10
Salt Lake City UT	7:10

Times From Cities & Towns To Telluride	
(Hours : Minutes)	
Denver	7:00
Grand Junction	2:55
Durango	2:20
Pagosa Springs	3:40
Cortez	1:30
Gunnison	3:10
Ouray	1:10
Moab UT	2:30
Salt Lake City UT	6:30

INTRODUCTION

The San Juans are an amazing, year-round alpine playground. Its main centers of ice climbing are located in or near the towns of Telluride, Ouray, and Silverton. This guide emphasizes these centers, with light coverage of the outlying areas of Durango, Lake City and Wolf Creek Pass.

The featured routes are pretty much roadside attractions. That said, snow often closes many of the roads leading to these routes, making the approaches much longer. There are many fine alpine ice climbs in the San Juans as well. These routes are usually in condition in the fall and the spring. A small selection of the best of these routes is mentioned here (expect the routes to be thin, mixed, and difficult).

Most climbs featured in this book are on public lands, but there are some on private land that have access issues so each route description has a land status indication. A worthy (and welcome) note: As of the printing of this book, Bridal Veil Falls, Telluride is legal to climb. See page 22 for more.

AVALANCHE DANGER

Avalanches are the greatest natural hazards facing climbers in the San Juan mountains. A working knowledge of avalanche forecasting and rescue techniques is required to travel safely in these mountains. Avalanche transceivers and shovels should always be carried on backcountry trips. You should not enter the backcountry without finding out what the local avalanche forecast says about current conditions. The local radio station (KOTO-fm Telluride / 89.5 / 91.7 / 105.5) broadcasts the Colorado Avalanche Information Center's latest report for the southern San Juans. You can also visit: http://avalanche.state.co.us.

SEASON

The water ice climbs of the San Juan mountains can come into condition as early as late October—particularly the perennial streams in the high country. Steep frozen waterfalls tend to be at their best in mid-winter (January and February), while snowmelt climbs are at their best in late winter (March and April). The season usually ends abruptly in the spring with a warm spell bringing the ice down in a real hurry. The few alpine routes in this guide are usually at their best from April to June. If you go into the backcountry in the spring and early summer, bring an axe and crampons. Snow can persist into summer months during years with exceptionally high snowfall.

GRADES

In the previously published words of Charlie Fowler, "grades don't mean shit." There is some truth to that, but with respects to water ice there are some very distinct characteristics that can be observed which lead well to the following grades for water ice (WI).

WI1

Walking where you only need crampons. A gently sloping frozen stream is a good example.

WI2

A steeper walk, but a hand tool can be of use. Example: Lower Fall Creek, Ouray.

WI3

Short sections of steep ice will be encountered. Required: crampons and two hand tools. Example: Lower Ingram Creek, Telluride.

WI4

Longer sections of steep ice (two to three body lengths) with an occasional stance for a rest and to place protection). Example: Second Gully, Eureka.

WI5

Sustained sections of vertical ice. Stances are rarely encountered. Protection is placed while hanging on tools. Example: Ames Ice Hose, Telluride.

WI6

Overhanging sections of ice should be expected or vertical ice in rotten condition—protection is virtually nonexistent and placing it can cost a lot of energy. Example: Bird Brain Boulevard, Camp Bird Mine Area.

Warning! Ice is plastic and in a state of constant flow or very slow movement. Warming temperatures increase the speed of this flow. Conditions are always changing. Rotten ice can be encountered on all grades which can turn a comfortable adventure into a epic. Please use good judgment. Climbing is dangerous and can be fatal. Climb at your own risk. The information in this book is for reference only and can not replace good judgment. Your use of this book in no way guarantees your personal safety.

HOT TIPS

• Most climbs in this book can be approached on foot although skis or snowshoes are sometimes useful.
• The best way to descend most routes is by rappelling. Remember to bring anchors and extra webbing that you can leave behind.
• There is a lot of private land in the areas covered in this book. Ice climbing is generally tolerated; please be discreet and respectful, and leave no trace.
• Climbers have created problems by parking along roadsides that must be kept clear in order for snowplows to do their job. Please take the parking suggestions seriously.
• Many climbs in the San Juan Mountains become drippy and wet. Dress accordingly.
• A light alpine rack, including pitons, can be useful. Eight to ten ice screws for protecting the pitch and at least two more for the anchor are recommended.
• Carry your V-Thread kit. If you don't have one, get one going.
• Leading ice climbs is for experts only—no foolin'.
• Many routes in this guide go by different names. Generally, names of routes conform with topographical features found on USGS maps. Many of the route names were made up by the author of the earlier editions. In this case, Charlie Fowler et al.

LEGEND

paved road
(with designation)

dirt road

trail

RR / Rail Road Tracks

left facing corner

right facing corner

ledge

roof

chimney

XX fixed anchor

face climbing

cliffband

Belay

**major descent
path/fixed
anchor**

tree

22 Route #

Δ Camping

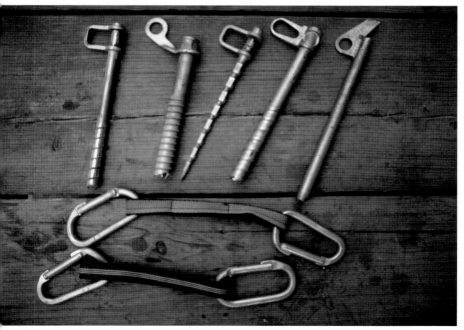

TELLURIDE

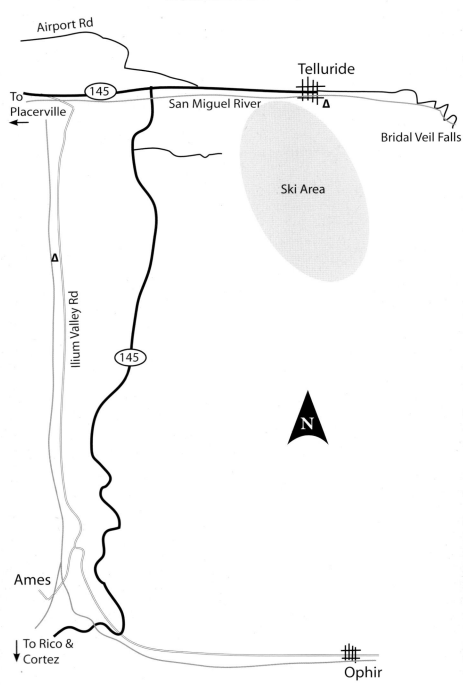

Airport Rd

Telluride

145

To Placerville

San Miguel River

Bridal Veil Falls

Ski Area

Ilium Valley Rd

145

N

Ames

To Rico & Cortez

Ophir

THE CLIMBING

The choices of ice climbs in the Telluride area are many. Climbers can find just about any level of difficulty and length, from short sixty-foot high WI3 to WI5 top-rope areas to long, multi-pitch routes like the famous Ames Ice Hose (WI5, 600').

HISTORY

Telluride, Colorado is one of the most stunning alpine towns anywhere and has played an important role in the evolution of ice climbing. In the winter of 1974, Jeff Lowe and Mike Weis made the first ascent of Bridal Veil Falls. At the time, it was regarded as the most difficult water ice climb in North America. It was given the grade of WI6 and it forever changed the way the alpinist looked at what could be climbed. Four years later, Lowe returned to Bridal Veil Falls and soloed it. Not only had he climbed the hardest water ice climb to date, he had climbed it in the purest style.

SEASON

Thanksgiving to just before the holiday season offers good early season ice climbing conditions. From the beginning of January to the second week in February is the best time to climb in the Telluride area, although the season will last until the end of March to the beginning of April. Depending on snowfall, several of the high alpine routes continue to be in good shape through May into early June.

PLACES TO STAY

For the visiting climber, accommodations in and near Telluride run the gamut from camping to luxurious. Without reservations, lodging can be difficult to obtain during the height of the ski season so book ahead if possible. Winter camping is limited but available. There are Forest Service lands at your disposal and they are indicated by the camping symbol on the Telluride Area map (p. 10).

LOCAL AREA SERVICES

Telluride is a lively little town. There's usually an abundance of cultural events and live music to pick from, making for a decent nightlife if the climbing doesn't take it out of you. There are a lot of fine places to eat and plenty of shops that will gladly take your money. For more information I recommend visiting the town's official website: www.visittelluride.com.

PARKING

Parking in Telluride has gotten better since the 1996 edition. The public parking area, Carhenge, is located south of the west end of San Juan Ave (map on p. 13). From the parking lot you can walk into town (under 10 minutes) or hop on the Galloping Goose bus loop (one of the buses runs on restaurant grease!). Main Street (Colorado Ave.) is metered parking, free on Sundays. Side street parking is either metered or requires a permit. Read all signage carefully as the town's plowing schedule will be in effect, closing certain sides on certain days. FYI: A parking ticket in Telluride is $20 to $40 a pop and parking in the plow zone will get you towed (well over $100).

MEDICAL SERVICES
The Telluride Medical Center is located at 500 W. Pacific Avenue. (970-728-3848). FYI: The Institute for High Altitude Medicine, founded in 2007 is at the same location.

WHAT TO DO WHEN YOU ARE NOT CLIMBING
The ski area is an attractive alternative when avalanche danger precludes ice climbing. The desert (a one to two hour drive from Telluride) offers great rock climbing most weeks of the winter months. Guidebooks for the nearby desert areas—"The Wild Wild West" (rock climbing) and "The Telluride & West End Bouldering Guide"—are available in most climbing shops in the region and on Telluride's main drag at Between The Covers Bookstore, which also offers coffee, couches and free wi-fi. In addition, the Wilkinson Public Library at offers free wi-fi and lots of computers for checking in with family and friends (www.telluridelibrary.org).

FA of Secret Steps, WI4, 150' / © Dan Gos

TOWN OF TELLURIDE

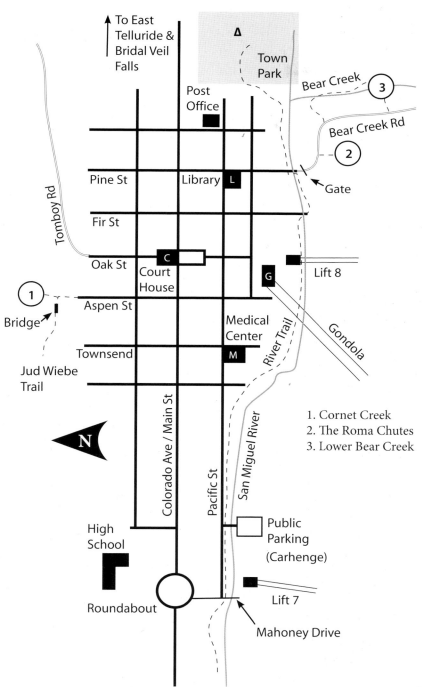

To East Telluride & Bridal Veil Falls

Town Park

Bear Creek

Bear Creek Rd

Post Office

Tomboy Rd

Pine St

Library

Gate

Fir St

Oak St

Court House

Lift 8

Bridge

Aspen St

Medical Center

River Trail

Gondola

Jud Wiebe Trail

Townsend

N

Colorado Ave / Main St

Pacific St

San Miguel River

1. Cornet Creek
2. The Roma Chutes
3. Lower Bear Creek

High School

Public Parking (Carhenge)

Roundabout

Lift 7

Mahoney Drive

CORNET CREEK

❑ **1. Cornet Creek** (map on p.13)
Grade: WI4 to 5
Height: 100'
Approach: 15 minutes from downtown
Avalanche Danger: Low
Land Status: National Forest
Best Season: Best climbed immediately after a cold spell (late December - January) a
the top melts out on warm-sunny days. Rare to find this climb in good shape late in
the season.

Cornet Creek is a popular classic pillar climb. The top is often wet and mixed. Bring
some thin hands to finger sized rock protection that may allow you to protect the top
out. It is also possible to top-rope this climb by walking around to the right (east) and
up the steep slope. There are very large trees from which to build a safe anchor. Walk
off or rappel from trees.

BEAR CREEK

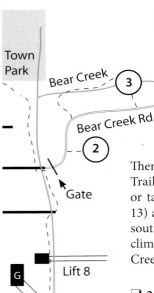

There are three climbing areas accessible from the Bear Creek
Trail (the trail follows the old road). Park at Carhenge, walk
or take the bus to the library (Town of Telluride map on p
13) and turn right on Pine St. (east side of the library). Head
south two blocks over the river. From the dead end of Pine St
climb a short steep hill and pass the entrance gate into the Bear
Creek Preserve Trail.

❑ **2. The Roma Chutes**
Grades: WI3 to 4
Height: 30' to 40'
Approach: 15 minutes from downtown
Avalanche Danger: Low to high
Land Status: National Forest
Best Season: Early to mid winter

Climb the short ice that forms on the left side of the cliff. Walk
off or rappel from trees.

❏ 3. Lower Bear Creek

Grades: WI3 to 5
Height: 80'
Approach: 30 minutes from downtown
Avalanche Danger: Low
Land Status: National Forest
Best Season: Early to mid winter

This route can be accessed two ways depending on the type of climbing you want to do. You can approach the cliff from the top and set up a top-rope or you can go down into and up the creek bed and come in below the ice climbs and lead the 80 or so feet of ice (in shape most of the winter). This is a superb practice area for all levels and abilities.

❏ 4. Upper Bear Creek Falls

Grades: WI3 to 4
Height: 100'
Approach: 59 minutes from downtown
Avalanche danger: Low to extreme; fortunately, the more desirable climbing is in the lower canyon where it is well protected from such danger.
Land Status: National Forest
Best Season: Early to mid winter

There are several ways to climb this 100' high slab of ice. Thin but protectable. Rappel from trees. Bring some extra webbing to back up any anchors tied around trees.

The thin, mixed exit on Lower Royer / © Chris Logan

MILL CREEK

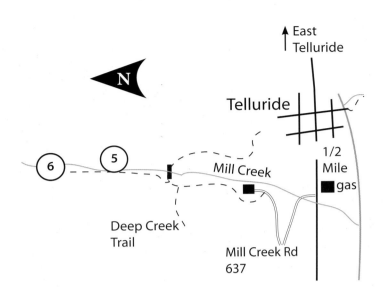

❏ 5. Lower Mill Creek Falls
Grade: WI4 to 5
Approach: 45 minutes
Height: 60'
Land Status: National Forest
Avalanche Danger: Low to moderate
Best Season: Mid-winter

❏ 6. Upper Mill Creek Falls
Grade: WI 4
Height: 180'
Approach: 1 hour
Land Status: National Forest
Avalanche Danger: Low to moderate
Best Season: Mid-winter

Drive west out of Telluride about one mile and make a right onto the Mill Creek Rd
(Just past the gas station.) Continue up the road until you dead end at the water treat-
ment plant. The Mill Creek trail head is on the left before the plant. The main icefall is
done in two pitches; one long, one short. Descent: 50m rappel from trees to left.

EAST TELLURIDE

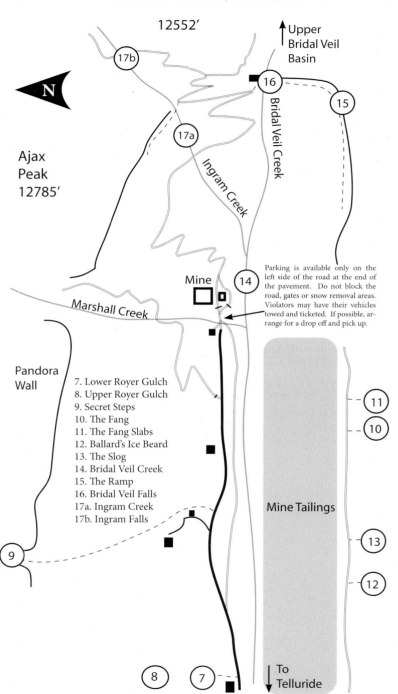

12552'

17b

N

↑ Upper
Bridal Veil
Basin

16

15

Ajax
Peak
12785'

17a

Ingram Creek

Bridal Veil Creek

Mine

14

Marshall Creek

Parking is available only on the left side of the road at the end of the pavement. Do not block the road, gates or snow removal areas. Violators may have their vehicles towed and ticketed. If possible, arrange for a drop off and pick up.

Pandora
Wall

7. Lower Royer Gulch
8. Upper Royer Gulch
9. Secret Steps
10. The Fang
11. The Fang Slabs
12. Ballard's Ice Beard
13. The Slog
14. Bridal Veil Creek
15. The Ramp
16. Bridal Veil Falls
17a. Ingram Creek
17b. Ingram Falls

11

10

Mine Tailings

9

13

12

8

7

↓ To
Telluride

17

A few comments about this area. First, there is a lot of private land in this area. The mine is still an active player in the east end of Telluride and continues to hold several mining claims (so many it makes your eyes cross looking at them on a map). Please be respectful of posted areas as it could jeopardize access to climbs. Secondly, Bridal Veil Falls is now legal to climb. As always, there are rules to abide by. They are listed in the Bridal Veil Falls section on p. 20.

❏ 7. Lower Royer Gulch
Grade: WI4
Height: 120'
Approach: 10 minutes
Land Status: National Forest, but approach crosses private land; obey posted signs
Avalanche Danger: Low to moderate, can be high when there is excessive snow
Best Season: Mid-winter

This is a very fun ice climb. Most parties only do the first pitch but there is exciting climbing above. Conditions can be thin during warm periods. Access is sensitive.

❏ 8. Upper Royer Gulch
Grade: WI4
Height: 200'
Approach: 1 hour
Land Status: National Forest
Avalanche Danger: Low to moderate, can be high when there is excessive snow
Best Season: Mid-winter

This route is comprised of two steep steps in a large gully. You can top out on Tombo Rd. and walk back to town (left or downhill) or you can rappel.

❏ 9. Secret Steps
Grade: WI4 (Run-out)
Height: 150'
Approach: 1 hour
Land Status: Public land but crosses private land; obey posted signs
Avalanche Danger: Low to moderate, can be high when there is excessive snow
Best Season: Mid-winter—after a long cold spell. FA was done in late January.

This route is located one mile east of Telluride on the left (north) side of the road. There is a long hike involved in this undertaking. You must climb about 1000' of steep (often covered with snow) hillside. Skis or snowshoes are recommended. This route is very thin in the beginning and offers little protection for the first 60' or so.

❏ 10. The Fang (a.k.a Acid Bath)
Grade: WI5
Height: 80'

Approach: 30 minutes

Land Status: National Forest but to approach this route by crossing the very large mine tailings is trespassing on Idarado Mining Company property. Idarado employees have called the authorities about climbers who make their way across the mine's property—hard to hide your footprints in the snow.

Avalanche: Low to moderate

Best Season: Mid-winter

Located just over a mile from town, this is Telluride's classic strenuous pillar route. You can often find a rest about three-fourths of the way up on the right. Descent: Rappel from trees or hike off (a steep bushwhack).

11. The Fang Slabs

Grade: WI2-3

Height: 60'

Approach: 30 minutes

Land Status: National Forest but to approach this route by crossing the very large mine tailings is trespassing on Idarado Mining Company property. See climb #10.

Avalanche: Low to moderate

Best Season: Most of the winter

These are fun short slabs. There are other slabs a bit longer and easier to approach—the Lower Ames Falls is an example. Descent: Rappel from trees.

12. Ballard's Ice Beard (a.k.a North Face of Ballard)

Grade: WI3 to 5

Height: 800' (including the long streamed WI1 to 2)

Approach: 1 hour

Land Status: National Forest but crosses private land; obey posted signs

Avalanche: Moderate to high, depending on snow conditions

Best Season: Mid-winter

Just about a half mile east of town, across the mine tailings deposit, if you look up to the south you will see ice that forms many potential routes. The main, obvious cliff is by far the most popular climb. This route climbs a long WI2 streamed to the base of the WI4 difficulties—two or three pitches up the narrow gully (chimney like at times). A harder variation exists to the right (WI5) finishing up a rock corner. Two other WI3 climbs can be found to the left (east) of the main climb. Descent: bushwhack west to Bear Creek and down old trails.

13. The Slog

Grade: WI5 – mixed (M5), A1

Height: 200'

Approach: 55 minutes

Land Status: National Forest but crosses private land; obey posted signs

Avalanche: Moderate to high, depending on snow conditions

Best Season: Mid winter, January

This route has only been climbed once that I am aware of. It comes in very rarely; have seen it in climbing shape twice in the last twelve years! About a quarter mile eas of Ballard's Ice Beard is a large arch-like overhang over which forms a WI5 ice dagger that does not reach the ground. Begin by climbing the very thin right corner up to th overhang. Traverse left (east) over mixed terrain to the thin ice blobs that ooze from the wall (thick enough for a 16cm screw or two). The roof is protected by two bolt and a pin—A1—which lead you to the dagger (WI5) for 100' into the trees. Descent Rappel trees.

❏ 14. Bridal Veil Creek
Grade: WI4
Height: 200'
Approach: 30 minutes
Land Status: National Forest
Avalanche: Moderate to high, depending on snow conditions
Best Season: Early winter, before snow covers most of the streambed

Climb the short stems of ice. Descent: Walk off left to road.

❏ 15. The Ramp
Grade: WI5 (mixed)
Height: 500'
Approach: 1 hour +
Land Status: National Forest
Avalanche: Moderate to high, depending on snow conditions
Best Season: Late winter

Climb the obvious ramp to the right of Bridal Veil Falls. Bring rock gear. Descent: Wal off left towards the power plant (but do not go near the building—private land—acces the road and descend back to the parking area).

❏ 16. Bridal Veil Falls
Grade: WI5 to 6
Height: 400'
Approach: 1 hour
Land Status: Public—Now Legal to climb!
Avalanche: Moderate to high on slopes around and to the east of the ice climb
Best Season: Most of the winter

This route is normally climbed in three pitches.
Pitch 1: Climb up the often cauliflower ice slab to the base of the vertical ice.
Pitch 2: The crux pitch. Climb the steep ice to the overhang—once past this section belay on sloping ice ledge.

Pitch 3: Climb up lower angle ice to the top of the route.
Descent: Rappel route. No upward exit. DO NOT trespass on the powerhouse property! The top anchors are just up stream about 30' on the left sides of the creek. (There is a set of anchors to the right, however, the left anchor is better for pulling your ropes).

Warning! Do not climb the ice routes to the left of the main climb—there are electrical cables running through them—sticking a tool into an electric cable could put a rather unpleasant end to your climbing career.

BRIDAL VEIL FALLS TOPO

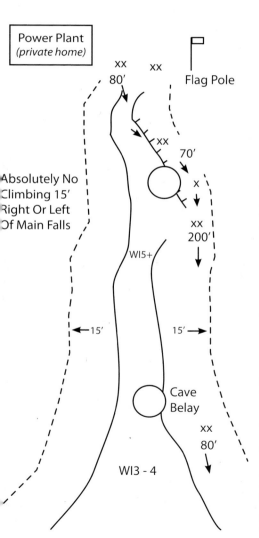

Special thanks to Idarado Mining Company, the Trust for Public Land and San Miguel County for helping to restore climbing access to Bridal Veil Falls, and to the Telluride Mountain Club. The Access Fund for promoting education and advocacy for climbing access.

Rappel anchors: There are several existing anchors to the right of the ice climb. These are for **rappel only**: two 60 meter ropes are required! They can be snow covered!

21

BRIDAL VEIL FALLS RECREATIONAL EASEMENT

The public recreational access license to the Bridal Veil Falls ice flow that San Miguel County currently hold is revocable, and any abuses of this area, or other violations of the license agreement between San Migue County, the Trust for Public Land and the Idarado Mining Company, could result in a climbing closure to the public. Please respect this area and it's access rules. ***Climbers must avoid the Powerhouse area at the top of Bridal Veil Falls.*** Descent route is via bolted anchors right of climb (see route map). Warning: The ap proach and descent for the Bridal Veil Falls ice flow will expose climbers to potentially hazardous avalanch terrain. Consult with local climbers and guides as to avalanche and route conditions before entering License Area (see route map). Bridal Veil Falls ice flow is an extremely difficult and dangerous climb and should be attempted only by experts. Beware of bad ice conditions and ice fall from natural causes or from other climb ers. Climbers assume any and all risks associated with climbing of the Bridal Veil Falls ice flow, an inherently dangerous activity that can result in serious injury or death. San Miguel County does not extend any assur ances to climbers or other members of the public that the Bridal Veil Falls ice flow is safe for ice climbing o any other purpose, nor does the County assume any responsibility for any injury to persons or property o for the death of any person caused by any act or omission of such person. Emergencies: In the event of emer gency call 911. Climbers are expected to be self reliant and perform self-rescue if necessary. Don't expect res cue or medical services to be immediately available or available at all. Climbers are encouraged to purchase a Colorado Hunting/Fishing License, or a COSAR Hiking Certificate in order to help reimburse San Migue County for potential rescue expenses. These are available at all Telluride outdoor retail stores.

RULES

1. REGISTRATION: Climbers must sign in and sign out at this register, and include date and time of day This helps keep track of how many climbers are using the area. It also lets other climbers know when a part is ahead of them, as well as assists in any potential rescue efforts. Climbers who do not register are considered to be trespassing.

2. GUIDES: Professional guides are required to complete a registration/release form available online at www sanmiguelcounty.org on the Open Space and Recreation page under Departments; or available from the Sa Miguel County offices located at 333 W. Colorado Avenue, 3rd Floor, in Telluride. All guides must posses and present acceptable evidence of liability insurance that names Idarado Mining Company, Trust for Publi Land, San Miguel County, or others as additional insureds. The minimum policy amount is $150,000 pe person, $600,000 per occurrence.

3. PROTECTION: Any ice and/or rock protection (other than used for retreat) must be removed. Climber must be properly equipped with appropriate gear while climbing and descending.

4. ACCESS: Access to the license area is limited to County Road K69. If you leave the county road, you ar trespassing on private property.

5. ROUTES: Climbers must restrict climbing and descending to the main Bridal Veil Falls and within 15 fee to either side. Climbers must descend the falls, or next to the falls via the bolted anchors (see topo for descer anchor locations). Climbers are not to enter into areas located outside of the designated climbing and descen routes. Climbing the ice east of the main Bridal Veil Falls (including anywhere under the powerhouse) i prohibited, as high-voltage electric and septic lines from the hydropower plant are located in the vicinity Climbing on nearby privately-owned cliffs is also prohibited.

6. POWERHOUSE: Climbers must avoid any interference with or trespassing on the powerhouse area. Climb ers must avoid touching or belaying off of any structure, fence, flume, porch or any other human improvemen in the License Area. Such improvements, including old bolts or trestle, may be unsafe and can break.

7. TOP-ROPING: Top-roping from the top of Bridal Veil Falls is prohibited.

PARKING: Parking is available only on the left side of the road at the end of the pavement. Do not block th road, gates or snow removal areas. Violators may have their vehicles towed and ticketed. If possible, arrang for a drop off and pick up.

INFORMATION SOURCES: Access changes, avalanche conditions, route and guide information is avail able at local outdoor retail stores in Telluride, as is the guidebook, San Juan Ice Climbs. The Colorado Ava lanche Information Center can be reached at (970)387-5712 or http://avalanche.state.co.us/.

GENERAL: Climbing access to Bridal Veil Falls is made possible by a revocable license agreement grante by the Idarado Mining Company to the Trust for Public Land and San Miguel County. Compliance wit these rules and regulations is necessary in order for climbing privileges to be maintained. The access agree ment is for a one-year term, subject to renewal, and can be revoked. Please treat this area and its adjacer private land with respect and help to educate others as to its proper use.

Steve Johnson on the FA of Ingram Falls / © Charlie Fowler

❏ 17a. Ingram Creek
Grade: WI3 to 4
Height: 500' (mostly walking on frozen streambed with occasional steep sections)
Approach: 40 minutes
Land Status: National Forest
Avalanche: Moderate to extreme
Best Season: Early winter

This streambed is normally the approach to the upper and more strenuous Ingram Falls, but is a fun outing in itself. Descent: Scramble down the streambed or walk off right. Note: Avalanche danger on the upper slopes, above the summer access road, can be extreme.

❏ 17b. Ingram Falls
Grade: WI5+
Height: 200'
Approach: 1.3 hours
Land Status: National Forest
Avalanche: Moderate to extreme; use extra caution if you walk off to the right (the summer access road)
Best Season: Mid to late winter

This is one of the most classic pillar routes in the area. The main pillar connects only occasionally and is more likely to form up as the winter progresses. Most people climb this route in one long pitch; therefore, a 70m rope will be useful. There is also a slab route to the left of the main pillar that offers fun early season climbing (WI4). To the right of the main pillar is a nice ice corner route that goes at WI5 and is normally climbed in two pitches—you may encounter mixed conditions.

Chris Straka aiding the 13' roof on The Slog / © Damon Johnston

24

EAST TELLURIDE (ALPINE)

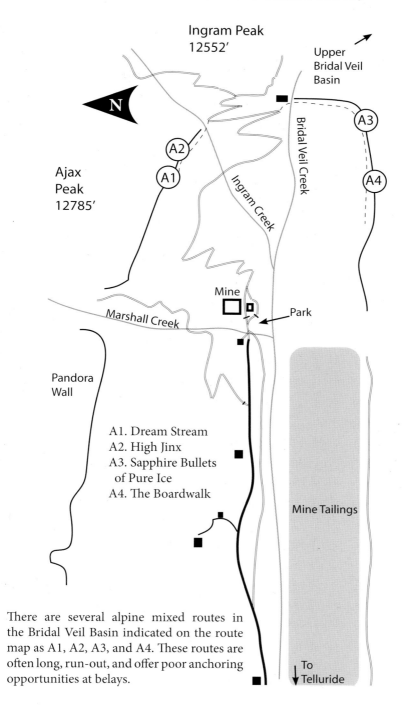

Ingram Peak
12552'

Upper
Bridal Veil
Basin

N

A2

A1

Ajax
Peak
12785'

Ingram Creek

Bridal Veil Creek

A3

A4

Mine

Marshall Creek

Park

Pandora
Wall

A1. Dream Stream
A2. High Jinx
A3. Sapphire Bullets
of Pure Ice
A4. The Boardwalk

Mine Tailings

There are several alpine mixed routes in
the Bridal Veil Basin indicated on the route
map as A1, A2, A3, and A4. These routes are
often long, run-out, and offer poor anchoring
opportunities at belays.

To
↓ Telluride

❏ A1. Dream Stream

Grade: WI5
Height: 1000' +
Approach: 1+ hour
Land Status: National Forest
Avalanche Danger: Low to moderate
Best Season: Mid-winter

This is the beautiful, curving chute directly below the summit of Ajax Peak when viewed from town. Usually, three or four pitches of ice lead to snow above. Descent: Rappel the route—the walk off to the left is epic! Variation to the left is WI4.

❏ A2. High Jinx

Grade: WI5
Height: 1000'+
Approach: 1+ hour
Land Status: National Forest
Avalanche Danger: Moderate to high
Best Season: Mid to late winter

The chute right of Dream Stream. A big pitch up high; to reach it may require a major approach if the lower pitches are dry.

❏ A3. Sapphire Bullets of Pure Ice

Grade: WI5
Height: 350'
Approach: 1+ hour
Land Status: National Forest
Avalanche Danger: Moderate to high
Best Season: Mid to late winter

Climb the deep, dark chimney system to the right of Bridal Veil Falls. This route is normally done in three pitches and offers some hard mixed climbing. There is a harder variation formed by a big steep pillar to the right in early spring. Descent: Walk off into the upper Bridal Veil Basin. Stay on the National Forest Service road.

❏ A4. The Boardwalk

Grade: WI4
Height: 1500'
Approach: 2+ hour
Land Status: National Forest
Avalanche Danger: Can be high to extreme
Best Season: Late winter to early spring

This route is easy to spot. Climb the major left leaning gully on the left flank of Ballard Mountain. Descent: Walk off left into Bridal Veil Basin—avalanche danger can be extreme.

UPPER BRIDAL VEIL BASIN

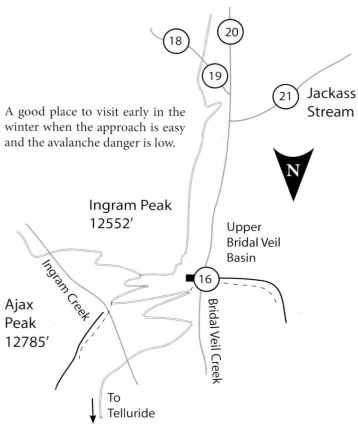

A good place to visit early in the winter when the approach is easy and the avalanche danger is low.

Jackass Stream

N

Ingram Peak
12552'

Upper
Bridal Veil
Basin

Ingram Creek

16

Ajax
Peak
12785'

Bridal Veil Creek

To
Telluride

AREA
Grades: 3 to 5
Heights: 20' to 70'
Approach: 1 hour+
Land Status: National Forest
Avalanche Danger: Low early in the season; can be moderate to extreme mid-season
Best Season: Late fall and very early winter

❑ **18. Upper Slab**, WI3, 70'.

❑ **19. Blue Lake Pillars** (a.k.a. The Main Area), WI4, 40' to 60'. Many short steep pillars form in this area.

❑ **20. Upper Bridal Veil Creek Streambed**, WI4 to 5, 20' to 70'. Many short steep steps that end at the top of a 70' chimney. Descent: Walk left to road and down.

❑ **21. Jackass Falls**, WI4, 400'. A super fun, early season climb—and worth the effort. The first two pitches are WI3 to 4. The rest is WI2 or so. Descent: Scramble down to the left of the falls.

DOWN VALLEY

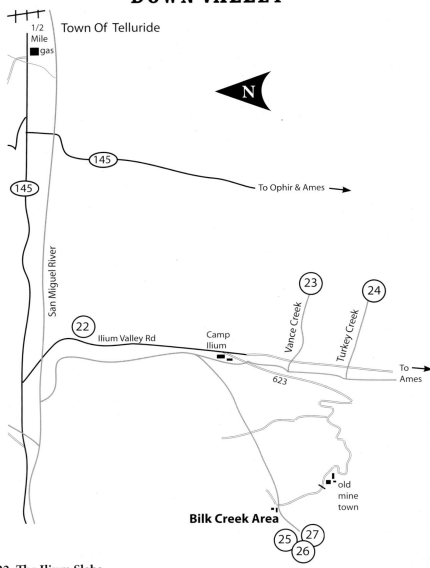

☐ **22. The Ilium Slabs**
Grade: WI3 and can form steep pillars—up to WI4
Height: 300'
Land: National Forest
Approach: 15+ minutes (from road)
Avalanche Danger: Low to moderate

This popular frozen streambed offers fun climbing for about 300 feet. Though this route is graded WI3, there can form steeper pillars that can be up to WI4.

❏ **23. Vance Creek Falls**
Grade: WI4
Height: 100' (depends on flow, can be smaller)
Approach: 15 minutes (from road)
Land: National Forest
Avalanche Danger : Low most of the time—seek out local avalanche forecast
Best Season: Mid winter

It is possible to see this route from HWY 145 but it is also easy to miss!

❏ **24. Turkey Creek Falls** (a.k.a Hidden Pillar)
Grade: WI4
Height: 100' or less
Approach: 15 minutes
Land: National Forest
Avalanche Danger: Low most of the time—seek out local avalanche forecast
Best Season: Mid winter

This route is visible from the Sunshine Mesa Road but is hidden from view down low. Hike up the streambed; you may need crampons up higher.

BILK CREEK

From Telluride, drive west down to the bottom of Keystone Hill (about 4.5 miles), make a left onto the Ilium Valley Road using the turn lane. Drive past the Sheriff's Department (watch your speed!) and continue on the road for 2 miles. Make a right onto 623 Road. Continue for 5.5 miles. Park at the old mine and hike past the gate, staying on the road. Pass between the two old buildings (a trailer and ragged shack) and continue hiking for 15 + minutes until the climbs come into view to the east.

❏ **25. 30-foot grade 3 pillar:** Starting here is the best way to approach the main falls

❏ **26. Bilk Creek Falls**
Grade: WI4
Height: 180'
Approach: 1 Hour +
Avalanche Danger: Extreme in mid winter
Best Season: Early season

❏ **27. Bilk Creek Slabs**
Grade: WI4/5
Height: 120'
Approach: 1 Hour +/-
Avalanche Danger: Extreme n mid winter
Best Season: Early season

The first 70 feet are steep and thin, many lines to choose from—some mixed!

DEEP CREEK

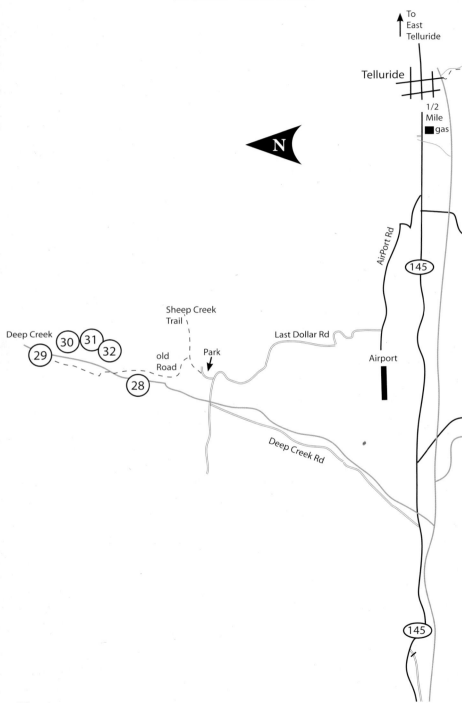

To
East
Telluride

Telluride

1/2
Mile
gas

AirPort Rd

145

Sheep Creek
Trail

Deep Creek

30 31
29   32
        28

old
Road

Park

Last Dollar Rd

Airport

Deep Creek Rd

145

N

Drive west on 145 out of Telluride for 5.5 miles. Deep Creek Road will be on your right. This dirt road will meet the Last Dollar Road in a couple of miles. Make a right at this intersection and look for the trail head on your left. Take the Sheep Creek Trail, then head left on the old road. Follow this old road until you see the climbs—about 40 minutes to 1 hour depending on which route you plan to climb.

❏ 28. Rocky Falls
Grade: WI4
Height: 100'+
Land Status: National Forest
Avalanche Danger: High in mid season
Best Season: Early season although conditions can last into the spring

This will be the first ice climb on your left. Descent: Rappel trees and Scramble.

❏ 29. Streambed
Grade: WI4
Land Status: National Forest
Height: 100'+
Avalanche Danger: High in mid season
Best Season: Early season although conditions can last into the spring

❏ 30. The Staircase
Grade: WI4
Height: 180'
Land Status: National Forest
Avalanche Danger: High in mid season
Best Season: Early season although conditions can last into the spring

❏ 31. Slab To Pillar
Grade: WI4 - 5
Height: 80'
Land Status: National Forest
Avalanche Danger: High in mid season
Best Season: Early season although conditions can last into the spring

❏ 32. Pillar To Gully
Grade: WI4 - 5
Height: 80'
Land Status: National Forest
Avalanche Danger: High in mid season
Best Season: Early season although conditions can last into the spring

DIAMOND HILL

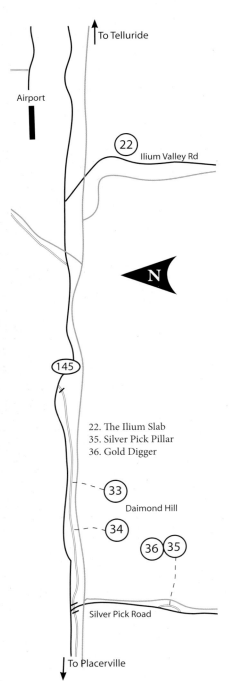

To Telluride

Airport

22

Ilium Valley Rd

N

145

22. The Ilium Slab
35. Silver Pick Pillar
36. Gold Digger

33

Daimond Hill

34

36 35

Silver Pick Road

To Placerville

These two streambed climbs can be seen from HWY 145 between the Ilium Valley turnoff and Silver Pick Road. Both of these routes require that you cross the San Miguel River, an easy task when it is frozen. Early and late season climbing may involve getting your feet wet. It is possible to use an aluminum extension ladder to make the crossing (28'). Park on the side of HWY 145, well out of the way of traffic.

❏ 33. Diamond Hill Streambed East
Grade WI3 to 4
Height: 400' +
Approach: 15+ minutes
Land Status: National Forest
Avalanche Danger: Low
Best Season: Early winter but can last into the spring

❏ 34. Diamond Hill Streambed West
Grade WI3 to 4
Height: 400'
Approach: 15+ minutes
Land Status: National Forest
Avalanche Danger: Low
Best Season: Early winter but can last into the spring

This is the better of the two streambeds.

ric Wright on the FA of Gold Digger, WI6 (M7/8) / Courtesy of Eric Wright.

There are several top-roping possibilities to the left of Silver Pick Pillar, which is just o the left of the photo above of Gold Digger. Bringing an extra rope to set up these op-rope climbs is helpful.

33

SILVER PICK

About 7 miles west of Telluride on the south side of HWY 145 turn left onto Silver Pick Road. Drive about one fourth of a mile and look for a place to park on the left side of the road—you can barely see part of the pillar from the road.

❑ **35. Silver Pick Pillar** (a.k.a The Sword)
Grade: WI5
Height: 80'
Approach: 15 minutes
Land Status: National Forest
Avalanche Danger: Low
Best Season: Most of the winter

This is a classic strenuous pillar for sure. Easy approach to very high quality climbing. Protection can be difficult. Descent: Rappel from trees. A 60m rope is a must and a 70m is better. Bring a very large sling (30') is you want to top-rope this route.

❑ **36. Gold Digger**
Grade: WI6 - M7 - 8
Height: 80'
Approach: 15 minutes
Land Status: National Forest
Avalanche Danger: Low

Best Season: Mid winter

This route starts on overhanging rock just to the left of the Silver Pick Pillar and continues up desperate thin daggers of ice and offers little protection. It can be top-roped easily—it is worth the time to set up. This route does have some fixed gear.

Climber leading the beginning of Silver Pick Pillar in thin conditions / © Eric Wright

PLACERVILLE

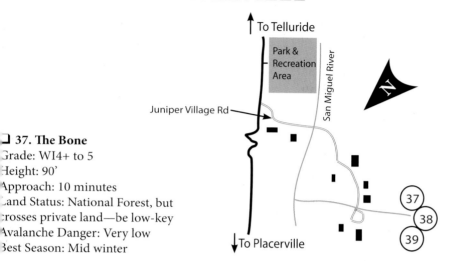

37. The Bone
Grade: WI4+ to 5
Height: 90'
Approach: 10 minutes
Land Status: National Forest, but
crosses private land—be low-key
Avalanche Danger: Very low
Best Season: Mid winter

This is the obvious pillar on the left. Climb pillar and belay from trees. Descent: Rappel from trees. WARNING! This climb can fall off in warmer temperatures. I once climbed the Three Elephants, rappelled The Bone, climbed Skull & Bones and was again setting up the rappel down The Bone when all of the sudden the ground shook and a very large ice-dust cloud filled the lower valley. The Bone, which we were about to rappel and then climb, had fallen off.

38. Skull & Bones
Grade: WI5 with a mixed top-out
Height: 90'
Approach: 10 minutes
Land Status: National Forest, approach crosses private land—be low-key
Avalanche Danger: Very low
Best Season: Mid winter or in cold spells

This route forms to the right of The Bone. Climb the thin ice and work your way over the top on rock. This route can be a challenge to protect. Descent: Rappel The Bone.

39. The Three Elephants
Grade: WI4
Height: 90'
Approach: 10 minutes
Land Status: National Forest, approach crosses private land—be low-key
Avalanche Danger: Very low
Best Season: Mid winter

Climb the far right ice climb that forms a cascading, trunk-like, feature. Descent: Rappel The Bone.

AMES

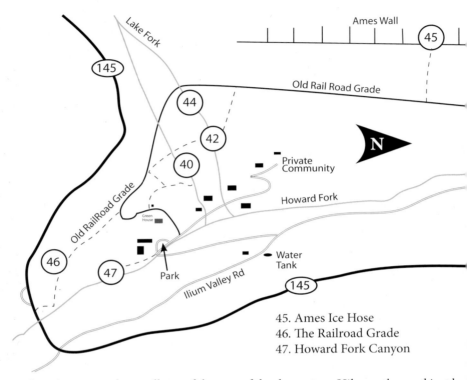

45. Ames Ice Hose
46. The Railroad Grade
47. Howard Fork Canyon

Park at the power plant well out of the way of the dumpsters. Hike up the road just be
yond the power plant building on the left. Pass the green house staying on the county
road—do not approach the house, it is private property. About 100' past the green
house the trail breaks off right at the old, mostly falling apart, cabin. Continue for about
200' where the trail splits. Right leads to the Lower Ames Falls Area. Left leads up to
the main Ames Falls. Stay left, climb the steep hill. Once on top, continue along the top
of the canyon staying right along the edge. A few minutes of hiking will bring you to a
right turn that crosses the top of the Lower Ames Falls, this will lead you to the top of
the main Ames Falls.

❏ 40. Lower Ames Falls
Grade: WI3
Height: 100'
Approach: 15 minutes
Land Status: National Forest
Avalanche Danger: Low
Best Season: All winter

This is a fabulous area to bring beginners and offers a fun warmup to the Upper Ames
Falls.

41. Lower Ames Falls Right (not on map)
Grade: WI4-
Height: 100'
Approach: 15 minutes
Land Status: National Forest
Avalanche Danger: Low
Best Season: All winter

This route is located just to the right of the main falls. It can be thin and often offers little protection.

42. Ames Falls Left (main falls)
Grade: WI4
Height: 150'
Approach: 20 minutes
Land Status: National Forest
Avalanche Danger: Low
Best Season: All winter

This is a very popular area for local climbers. It is possible to rappel from trees down into the canyon, pull your ropes and lead out. You can also lower your partner into the canyon and belay them up from the top.

43. Ames Falls Right (not on map)
Grade: WI5
Height: 100'
Approach: 20 minutes
Land Status: National Forest
Avalanche Danger: Low
Best Season: All winter

The most popular route in Ames. Climb the right side of the main falls. You can rappel from trees, pull your rope and lead out. Or you can set up a solid top-rope and rappel into the canyon—belaying from either the bottom or the top. An extra rope to tie off multiple trees is useful—or several very long runners.

44. Upper Ames Falls (a.k.a. Diana Falls)
Grade: WI4
Height: 50'
Approach: 30 minutes
Land Status: National Forest
Avalanche Danger: Low
Best Season: All winter

From the top of Ames Falls, walk up the stream about 10 minutes until you come to the obvious waterfall. Several variations exist. Descent: Rappel from trees.

❑ 45. Ames Ice Hose

Grade: WI5 to 6
Height: 600'
Approach: 1 hour
Land Status: National Forest
Avalanche Danger: Moderate to high
Best Season: All winter

Conditions on the approach and the climb vary drastically from year to year. This is one of the all-time classic San Juan ice climbs. Rock gear is a must when climbing this route! Descent: Rappel the route or walk off the left (not recommended).

From the top of the Ames Falls (main falls), hike up the steep slope just on the other side of the stream until you are on the old railroad grade. Turn right (north) and continue until you are under the Ames Ice Hose. Hike up the steep gully up to the base.

Pitch 1: This pitch is about 180 feet and can be super thin. There can be little protection here as well. If you want to spice things up, there is a mixed variation to the right.

Pitch 2: Continue up the ice-filled chimney mounting steep steps with occasional stances to place gear at their bases. Expect 200 feet. If conditions are thin, this pitch can be mixed in places.

Pitch 3: The upper headwall is often steep and thick.

When the snow pack is light it is possible to find additional pitches of ice above what is considered the final pitch of the Ames Ice Hose. Most people do not climb these upper pitches. There is also an ice climb to the north that forms up most years.

❑ 46. The Railroad Grade

Grade: WI3 to 5
Height: 50'
Approach: 10 minutes
Land Status: National Forest
Avalanche Danger: Low
Best Season: All winter
Special Gear: Top-rope, light rack

This can be a fun playground when if forms. It is easy to see this area from HWY 145 from the Ames turnoff. Several options exist, including some mixed climbing. Most people boulder or top-rope the routes from the trees above. Access fro the Ophir loop has been disputed.

AMES ICE HOSE

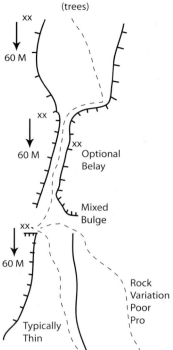

Alex Lowe soloing the Ames Ice Hose / © Charlie Fowler

❏ 47. Howard Fork Canyon

Grade: WI3 to 6
Height: 100'
Approach: 10 minutes
Land Status: National Forest
Avalanche Danger: Moderate to high
Best Season: Mid winter
Special Gear: A healthy rack will be needed to lead the mixed routes here

Several high quality routes exist in this canyon. Park at the Ames power plant (do not block access to any buildings). Hike up the creek about 10 minutes. The harder climbing is on the right side (south) of the canyon as you hike in from Ames. A few easier routes (WI3 to 4) can be found on the left (north) side of the canyon.

OPHIR

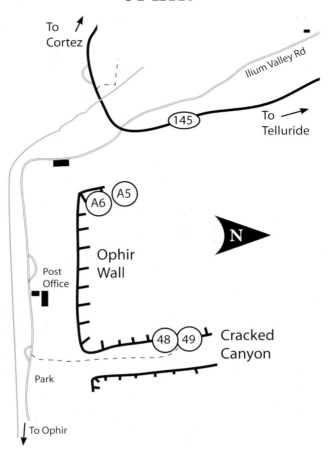

❑ **48. The Pencil**
Grade: WI5+ R/X
Height: 80'
Approach: 30+ minutes
Land Status: National Forest
Avalanche Danger: Low to moderate
Best Season: Mid winter

This extremely thin pillar that forms only in the best of years is located just to the left of the Crack Canyon Ice Pillar. There is virtually no protection. This pillar is so thin that you can nearly wrap your arms around it and it is often all candle ice. It is also detached until the last 10 feet or so. Spooky lead! On the bright side, there is a bolted anchor at the top.

❏ 49. Cracked Canyon Ice Pillar

Grade: WI4 to 5 (up to WI 6 if the start is mixed)
Height: 260'
Approach: 30+ minutes
Land Status: National Forest
Avalanche Danger: Low to moderate. Watch for rock fall!
Best Season: Mid winter
Rock Gear: Thin to wide hands

This is one of the best climbs in the area. Park on the right side of the road up the hill, east from the Post Office. Cross the road and hike up the snow covered talus field until you are in the canyon with rock on both sides of you. Continue almost to the top of the canyon. Look for the obvious ice on the left. You can see the climb from the parking area.

Pitch 1: In a good year, the 150' first pitch is all ice and connected to the ground (WI5). Most likely it will not and you will have to traverse in, protecting the route with rock gear, until you can sink your tools into good ice. There is an anchor up and to the right.

Pitch 2: Continue up the ice ramp and the steep headwall. Look for the very large pine tree from which to belay. 160', WI4+. Descent: Rappel the route.

❏ **A5**, Thin Mixed Corner, WI 5 to 6, 300', Descent: Rappel or walk left.

❏ **A6**, Snow Gully, WI4, climb several steps.

Alex Lowe on the Cracked Canyon Ice Pillar / © Charlie Fowler

WATERFALL CANYON

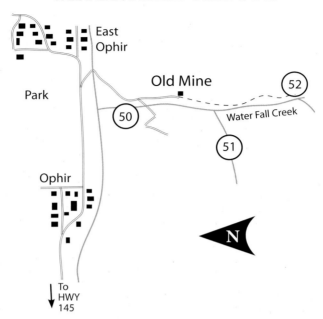

❏ 50. Lower Falls
Grade: WI4
Height: 50'
Approach: 25+ minutes
Land Status: National Forest
Avalanche Danger: Low to moderate
Best Season: Mid winter

❏ 51. Yellow Mountain Pillar
Grade: WI5
Height: 60'
Approach: 45 minutes
Land Status: National Forest
Avalanche Danger: High to extreme
Best Season: Late winter to early spring

❏ 52. Ulysses Flow
Grade: WI3 to 4-
Height: 60'
Approach: 1 hour+
Land Status: National Forest
Avalanche Danger: High to extreme
Best Season: Late winter to early spring
Special Gear: Skis are helpful

OURAY

The old mining town of Ouray has traditionally been the focal point of San Juan ice climbing. The proximity to many ice climbs as well as the hospitable community makes Ouray an attractive basecamp for visiting climbers.

Lodging is fairly plentiful in the winter and reasonably priced. It is necessary to make reservations if you are traveling to the Ouray Ice Festival which takes place yearly every January (www.ourayicefestival.com). There are several choices for eating and drinking; most of which are on the main drag. There are also several commercially operated hot springs offering a great way to relax after a day on the ice: Ouray Hot Springs (sorry no website, look for the first large pool of hot water on the right as you enter Ouray from the north) and the clothing-optional Orvis Hot Springs (www.orvishotsprings. com). Ouray also offers a full-service climbing shop located on Main St. Their website provides a good resource for local conditions and other related information (www. ouraysports.com). They also have a new ice screw sharpening machine!

Although there are several excellent long climbs in the area, Ouray is primarily known for its short routes. The Camp Bird area and the Uncompaghre Gorge (the Ouray Ice Park) attract more climbers than any other areas in the San Juans. The Ouray Ice Park is an excellent place to learn the craft of climbing ice and there are several guide services that operate in the area.

In this guidebook, the climbs in and around Ouray are split up into several sections: Ouray North, Dexter Creek, Ouray Ice Park, Camp Bird, Skylight, Birdbrain, Ouray South, Bear Creek, Gravity's Rainbow, Horsetail Falls, and more.

Pipeline over the School Room Area in the Ouray Ice Park / © Damon Johnston

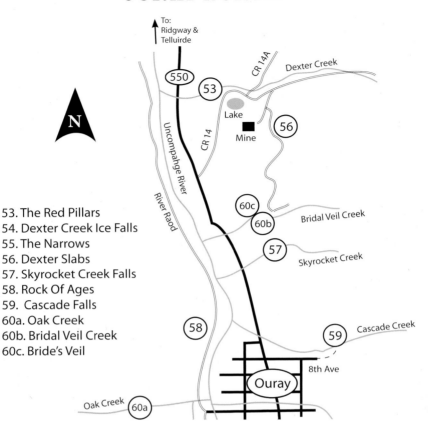

53. The Red Pillars
54. Dexter Creek Ice Falls
55. The Narrows
56. Dexter Slabs
57. Skyrocket Creek Falls
58. Rock Of Ages
59. Cascade Falls
60a. Oak Creek
60b. Bridal Veil Creek
60c. Bride's Veil

Dexter Canyon is a beautiful narrow canyon with many hard lines. These ice climbs can be in condition all winter long. Most of the time, the avalanche danger is low.

❏ **53. The Red Pillars**
Grade: WI5
Height: 200'
Approach: 20 to 30 minutes
Land Status: Private, has been closed in the past
Avalanche Danger: Low
Best Season: Most of winter
Special Gear: V-Thread or ability to make an ice bollard

Several WI5 pillars can exist here. These routes are often not formed to the top of the canyon. Rappel from ice bollards or V-Thread. The ice is stained a nice red from the iron minerals in the sandstone.

DEXTER CREEK

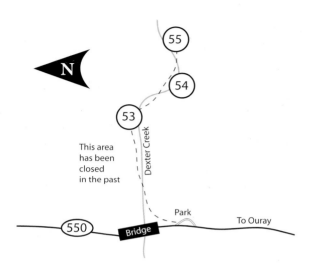

54. Dexter Creek Ice Fall (topo on p. 46)
Grade: WI4 to 5
Height: 200'
Approach: 30+ minutes
Land Status: Private, has been closed in the past
Avalanche Danger: Low
Best Season: Most of winter

55. The Narrows
Grade: WI4 to 5
Height: 200'
Land Status: Private, has been closed in the past
Avalanche Danger: Low
Best Season: Most of winter

Two additional climbs exist back where the canyon gets really narrow.

"Ice is for pouring whisky on."
— Tom Patey

DEXTER CREEK FALLS

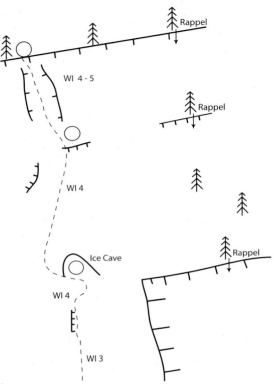

O
U
R
A
Y

❏ 56. Dexter Slabs
Grade: WI3 to 4
Height: 250'
Approach: 20 minutes
Land Status: National Forest
Avalanche Danger: Moderate
Best Season: Most of winter

This broad sheet of ice is a popular spot for beginners. Many moderate lines exist. Th
views are very nice. Descent: walk off left or rappel off trees.

❏ 57. Skyrocket Creek Falls
Grade: WI5
Height: 90'
Approach: 15+ minutes
Land Status: National Forest
Avalanche Danger: Moderate
Best Season: Mid winter

Includes a fun section of WI3 ice in the gully.

❏ 58. Rock Of Ages
Grade: WI4 to 5
Height: 200'
Approach: 10 or fewer minutes
Land Status: National Forest
Avalanche Danger: Low to moderate
Best Season: A spring snowmelt climb

This climb usually comes in late winter and early spring—only in some years. This route can be found north and above the hot springs.

❏ 59. Cascade Falls
Grade: WI4 to 5
Height: 300'
Approach: 15 minutes
Land Status: National Forest
Avalanche Danger: Low to moderate
Best Season: Mid winter

A classic, but rarely in good condition. Walk right and rap off trees. There is a pitch higher up.

❏ 60a. Oak Creek
Grade: WI4 to 5
Height: 200'
Approach: 20 minutes
Avalanche Danger: Low to moderate
Best Season: Mid winter

Another melt climb, rarely in good condition. There is an approach trail but the creek is a better option.

❏ 60b. Bridal Veil Creek
Grade: WI3 - 4
Height: 100'
Approach: 15 minutes
Land Status: National Forest
Avalanche Danger: Low to moderate
Best Season: Mid winter

❏ 60c. Bride's Veil
Grade: WI5
Height: 130'
Approach: 15 minutes
Land Status: National Forest
Avalanche Danger: Low to moderate
Best Season: Mid winter

OURAY ICE PARK

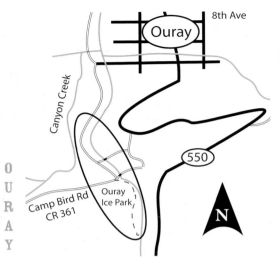

Olivija Berry, 7, enters the new kids area for the Kids College at the 2008 Ouray Ice Festival / © Daiva Chesonis

This is a very popular area, offering many steep climbs from 90' to 200' high. Routes are commonly top-roped (though sections of the Ice Park are "lead only" areas. Heavy traffic on an ice climb can lower the grade a lot. The Ice Park is split up into to several areas (listed on the Ice Park Areas Map on p. 50). Nowadays, there are signs pointing the way to all the areas. This guide will not include information on every route in every area. I have selected several of the best lines for this guide and cover some areas in a general way. For more detailed information on mixed climbing in the Ice Park please visit www.ourayicepark.com. WARNING! The Ice Park can become very busy, DO NOT hang out directly under the routes. Climbers may crack off small to very large chunks of ice that will crash down on unsuspecting climbers below. Once you are in the gorge a helmet is a must. Be smart and pay attention—stay out of harms way.

OURAY ICE PARK RULES & ETIQUETTE
1. Buy a membership, support your park.
2. Leave gear on an anchor if you are leading a route so that nobody will rappel onto you.
3. Use the walk downs to get to the base of the route if there is anyone below. This way you will not knock ice down onto them. Many accidents have been caused by this.
4. Yell real loud before you throw ropes into the gorge, or better yet, get a visual that nobody is on your route. It is very difficult to hear people in the gorge from above.
5. Do not take gear off of a route. If there are quick draws left on a route, then someone is projecting that route. Quick draws left on bolts is not abandoned gear and should be left in place. They may be there for a competition as well.
6. Be aware of people climbing above you if you are climbing or at the base of a route. Ice can fall a long way.

. Learn how to belay from the top of a route. Belay off the anchor rather than your harness.
. Crampons and helmets are required in the gorge.
. Don't take your dog into the gorge.

RULES OF THE OURAY ICE PARK

- CRAMPONS ARE REQUIRED FOR ALL PERSONS (CLIMBERS OR OTHERWISE) IN THE ESTABLISHED AND POSTED "CLIMBER ONLY" AREAS.
- CRAMPONS AND A HELMET ARE REQUIRED FOR ALL PERSONS WHILE CLIMBING OR IN THE BOTTOM OF THE GORGE.
- DO NOT OCCUPY MORE THAN TWO CLIMBING ROUTES IN ANY ONE SPECIFIC AREA. NO UNATTENDED FIXED TOP-ROPE LINES ALLOWED.
- PLEASE BE KIND AND WATCH YOUR TIME ON AN ANCHOR. THERE ARE OTHERS THAT WISH TO CLIMB.
- NO ANCHORING TO ANY MANMADE STRUCTURES INCLUDING THE PENSTOCK (THE BIG RED PIPE).
- ALL CLIMBING IN THE "SCHOOL ROOM" AREA MUST BE ON ESTABLISHED AND NUMBERED FIXED ANCHORS.
- IT IS SUGGESTED THAT ALL PERSONS UNDER THE AGE OF 18 BE ACCOMPANIED BY AN ADULT AT ALL TIMES.
- DOGS MUST BE LEASHED WHILE AT THE OURAY ICE PARK AND NO DOGS ARE ALLOWED IN THE BOTTOM OF THE GORGE.
- PERSONS VIOLATING THESE RULES WILL LOSE THE PRIVILEGE OF CLIMBING IN THE ICE PARK.
- PLEASE BE COURTEOUS AND RESPECT YOUR FELLOW CLIMBERS.

O
U
R
A
Y

Ouray Ice Festival Competition / © Charlie Fowler

OURAY ICE PARK

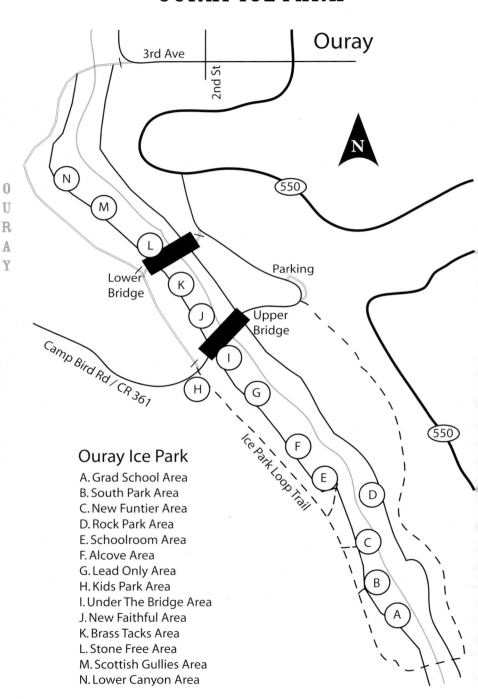

Ouray

3rd Ave

2nd St

N

550

N

M

L

Lower
Bridge

K

J

Parking

Upper
Bridge

Camp Bird Rd / CR 361

H

I

G

550

F

E

D

Ice Park Loop Trail

C

B

A

O
U
R
A
Y

Ouray Ice Park

A. Grad School Area
B. South Park Area
C. New Funtier Area
D. Rock Park Area
E. Schoolroom Area
F. Alcove Area
G. Lead Only Area
H. Kids Park Area
I. Under The Bridge Area
J. New Faithful Area
K. Brass Tacks Area
L. Stone Free Area
M. Scottish Gullies Area
N. Lower Canyon Area

NOTE: ALL AREAS AND ROUTES ARE LISTED LEFT TO RIGHT ... UPSTREAM TO DOWNSTREAM!

A. Grad School Area

Many moderate routes from WI 2 to 3 with an occasional 4. This is the furthest area from the bridge—it can take 20 minutes to access these routes from the road.

B. South Park Area

This area has many routes from WI2 to 5. Expect about a 10-minute walk from the bridge. Bring extra webbing and/or long slings for using the trees on top for anchors. There is usually a fixed rope on the trail down to this area.

C. New Funtier

This area is upstream from the Schoolroom Area. About 10 minutes from the road. This area has many moderate routes WI4 and below. This is a wonderful place to experience.

D. Rock Park

NO DRY TOOLING, rock climbing only. Several bolted sport routes are located on the sunny side of the gorge—it is possible to see several bolts and anchors on the face from the trail across the canyon. Rappel in from anchors.

❏ **Hail To The Thief**, 5.12b, 20m, bolts

❏ **Arms Race**, 5.11d, 100' bolts

❏ **Freedom Fighters**, 5.11a, 100', bolts

❏ **Jimmy's Arete**, 5.11a, 90', bolts

E. Schoolroom Area

❏ **Henhouse**, WI2, slab

❏ **Rooster's Roost**, WI3 to 4, slab will occasionally form a pillar

❏ **Schoolroom Pillar,** WI4 to 4+, there are a few ways to climb this route

❏ **Dean's List**, 5.11, 4 bolts, a bolted climb just downstream of the Schoolroom

❏ **Behind The Trestle Wall**, WI 4 to 5, a few possibilities exist here

F. Alcove Area

❏ **Wilford's Way**, mixed (M6 to 7), located on the right side of the Alcove

❏ **Verminator**, WI4, on the upstream side to the second arête

❏ **Duncan's Delight**, WI5, smear on the downstream side of the upstream arête

❏ **Paranoia**, WI4, located between the two arête. Find the exposed wall that offer some mixed climbing.

❏ **Pic'O The Vic**, WI4, the obvious sheet of ice visible from the upper bridge. Look for the tree sticking out of the wall.

O U R A Y

G. Lead Only Area
❑ **Tangled Up In Blue**, WI4 to 5, located just upstream form the upper bridge
❑ **Whitt's World**, WI4, just right of Tangled Up In Blue
❑ **Abridgment**, WI4, just right of Whitt's World

H. Kids Climbing Park
Located by the upper bridge and directly above the Lead Area is the new Kids Climbing Park, offering several top-rope options above the short WI2 to 3 blobs of ice.

I. Under The Upper Bridge (left to right)
❑ **Under The Boardwalk** (a.k.a Extreme Dream), WI5
❑ **Grandma's Glass Pony Shop**, WI6
❑ **No Doubt Spout**, WI 5

J. New Faithful Area (look for the yellow ice)
❑ **O'D On Ice**, WI5
❑ **Pale Ale**, WI5+
❑ **Root Canal**, WI6
❑ **LePissoir**, WI5
❑ **Chris' Crash**, WI5, hanging slab, with pin in cave. This route is a little way downstream from the above routes.

K. Brass Tacks
❑ *Many options*, WI4 to 5

L. Stone Free Area
❑ **Culminator**, WI5
❑ **Optimator**, WI5
❑ **Popsicle**, WI5 to 6
❑ **Stone Free**, WI5 to 6, right edge fixed pin and mixed.

M. Scottish Gullies
❑ *Mixed gullies*, WI3

N. Lower Canyon Area
❑ **LaVentana**, WI5+
❑ **Kaleidoscope**, WI4
❑ **Aqua Velva**, WI4

CAMP BIRD

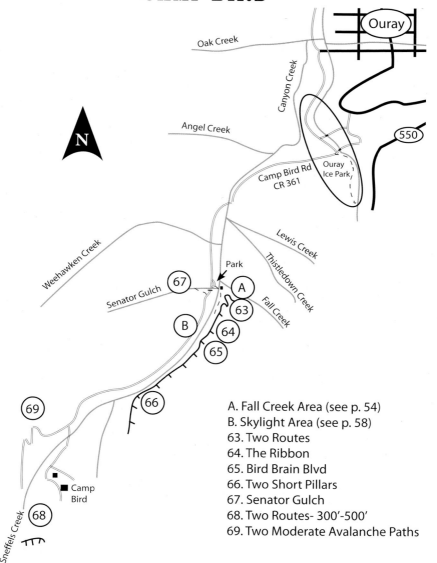

A. Fall Creek Area (see p. 54)
B. Skylight Area (see p. 58)
63. Two Routes
64. The Ribbon
65. Bird Brain Blvd
66. Two Short Pillars
67. Senator Gulch
68. Two Routes- 300'-500'
69. Two Moderate Avalanche Paths

The Camp Bird area is one of the most popular destinations in the region due to the variety and abundance of high quality climbs. Most climbs in this area form from snowmelt. As a result, they are usually at their best mid to late winter—though in years with early snowfall, it is possible to find some routes in shape earlier in the season. Note: Fall Creek Area and Senator Gulch Area are exposed to the sun and can become rotten quickly.

FALL CREEK

❑ **61. Mainline**
Grade: WI4
Height: 1000'
Approach: 50 minutes
Land Status: National Forest
Avalanche Danger: Moderate to extreme
Best Season: Early winter to avoid extreme avalanche danger
Special Gear: V-Thread (handy when the anchors are covered in ice), head-lamp

Mostly easy climbing. There are two short WI4 sections. Normally climbed in three pitches. Descent: Rappel the route. WARNING! The top of the this route is an avalanche gully. In times of heavy snow accumulation, this route can become extremely dangerous.

❑ **62. Out Of The Mainstream**
Grade: WI4 to 5
Height: 1200'
Approach: 50 minutes
Land Status: National Forest
Avalanche Danger: Moderate to extreme
Best Season: Early winter to avoid extreme avalanche danger
Special Gear: V-Thread (handy when the anchors are covered in ice), head-lamp

An excellent long climb that gets progressively more challenging as you climb higher—look to the right for the WI5 variation. Descent: Rappel the route. WARNING! The top of the this route is an avalanche gully. In times of heavy snow accumulation, this route can become extremely dangerous.

❑ **63. Two Routes**
Grade: WI4 to 5
Height: 1000'
Approach: 50 minutes
Land Status: National Forest
Avalanche Danger: Moderate to extreme
Best Season: Early winter to avoid extreme avalanche danger
Special Gear: V-Thread (handy when the anchors are covered in ice), head-lamp

At least two climbs have been done on this buttress. One, a large left-facing corner chimney on the left, WI4 to 5, 1000'. The other, the center crack/chimney system, WI4 to 5, 1000'. There is a lot of mixed climbing on both routes. Descent: Rappel the route.

MAINLINE & OUT OF THE MAINSTREAM

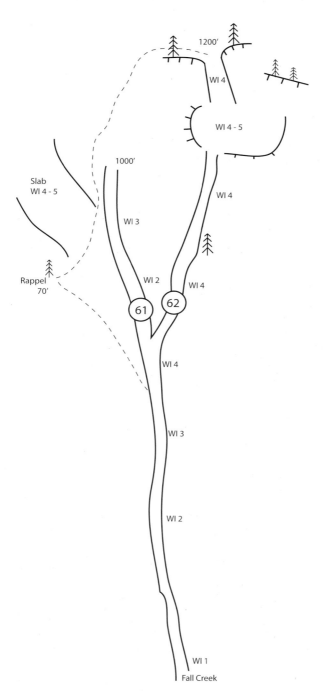

1200'

WI 4

WI 4 - 5

Slab
WI 4 - 5

1000'

WI 3

WI 4

Rappel
70'

WI 2

WI 4

61

62

WI 4

WI 3

WI 2

WI 1

Fall Creek

BIRD BRAIN BOULEVARD

❏ **64. The Ribbon**
Grade: WI4
Height: 600'
Approach: 30 minutes
Land Status: Private, observe posted signs
Avalanche Danger: Moderate to extreme
Best Season: Early winter to avoid extreme avalanche danger
Special Gear: V-Thread (handy when the anchors are covered in ice), head-lamp

A striking line that most parties do not top-out on. The top of this route is an avalanche gully—WARNING! In time of heavy snow accumulation, this route can become extremely dangerous—even a DEATH ROUTE. Descent: Rappel the route.

❏ **65. Bird Brain Boulevard**
Grade: WI5 to 6, with a section of hard mixed climbing up high
Height: 1000'
Approach: 40 minutes
Land Status: Private, observe posted signs
Avalanche Danger: Moderate to extreme
Best Season: Mid winter
Special Gear: V-Thread (handy when the anchors are covered in ice), head-lamp, extra warm clothing (in the shade at all times of the day). Rock Gear: thin to wide hands, a few long slings, 60m x 2, even a knife-blade or two can be handy.

Avalanche danger is fairly low on this climb, but the approach can be a different story—take care on the slopes below the climb. Descent: Rappel from trees off to the left of the route.

❏ **66. Two Short Pillars**, WI5, two to three pitches. In some years a couple of short thin lines form up here. WARNING: The approach is in dangerous avalanche terrain. Descent: Walk and scramble off to the right—may need to setup an occasional rappel.

❏ **67. Senator Gulch**
Grade: WI4 to 4+
Height: 100'
Approach: 10 minutes
Land Status: Private as posted
Avalanche Danger: Low
Best Season: Mid winter

❏ **68 Two Routes** (300 - 500'). There are two climbs in this area. The left climb is WI5, 300', two pitches up the pillar, and has a direct finish or a mixed variation to the right. The second climb (right) is WI5 to 6, 500', and climbs several short pillars and curtains. A wild climb for sure.

❏ **69. Two Moderate Avalanche Paths**, WI3 to 4. Fun, late fall or early winter climbs. Avoid mid winter.

56

BIRD BRAIN BOULEVARD TOPO

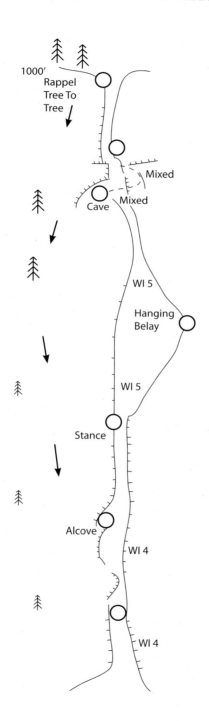

1000'
Rappel
Tree To
Tree

Mixed

Cave   Mixed

WI 5

Hanging
Belay

WI 5

Stance

Alcove

WI 4

WI 4

SKYLIGHT

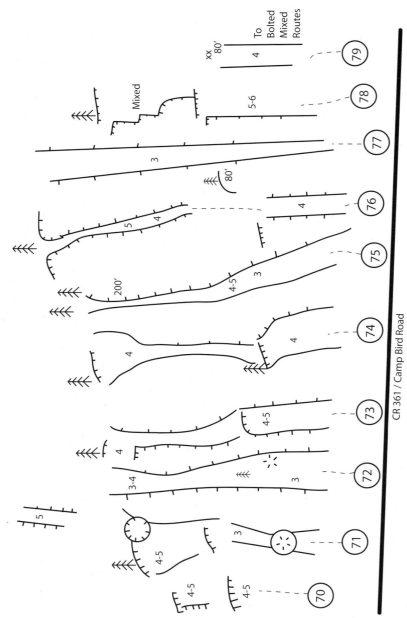

CR 361 / Camp Bird Road

These climbs range from 100' to 250' high. The avalanche danger can be extreme in times of bad snow conditions—check locally about conditions. Rock hardware is useful to protect many of these routes. You will almost always be rappelling form tree anchors. Bring extra webbing just in case you find the anchor in poor condition. A quick-link or two to leave at the anchor is also a good idea—rappelling directly from webbing should be avoided whenever possible.

Park below the gate which is closed most of winter, and out of the main road area. They plow the road often in winter. Hike up the road to the climbs about 10 minutes to the Skylight Area climbs passing several bolted mixed routes along the way.

☐ 70. **Thin Slice**, WI4 to 5, two short steep pitches, can be top-roped.

☐ 71. **Chockstone Chimney**, WI3 to 5. Easy if you stay to the right and harder variations (some mixed) can be found on the left. Descent: Rappel from trees or down climb easier sections.

☐ 72. **Chock Up Another One**, WI3 to 4. Two lines can be found here. Climb the left in the gully WI3—can be thin. Or stay right on short steep pillars—WI4.

☐ 73. **Slippery When Wet**, WI4 to 5, two pitches. Can be thin or mixed.

☐ 74. **Slip Sliding Away**, WI 4+, 2 pitches. A hard variation finishes right. First pitch can be top-roped from small trees above.

☐ 75. **Choppo's Chimney**, WI4 to 5, a popular route that is normally climbed in one pitch. 60m rope x 2. Descent: Rappel from large tree at top.

☐ 76. **The Skylight**, WI5, mixed, 2 pitches, bring rock gear. Short lower mixed pitch and one long pitch to the top.

☐ 77. **The Cleft**, WI3, easy ice up high.

☐ 78. **Road Warrior**, WI5 to 6, steep and thin, this climb rarely forms into good shape. Often only the first pitch is climbable.

☐ 79. **Roadside Attraction**, WI4, short.

RED MOUNTAIN PASS

Ouray

Oak Creek

Canyon Creek

Portland Cree

Δ

80

550

81

82

Camp Bird Rd
CR 361

Ouray
Ice Park

N

87

Park

84

Ralston Cr

86

Bear Creek

85

83

Uncompahge Gorge

88

89

550

90

91

92

93

Silver Gulch

94

Engineer
Pass Rd

W Riverside Slide

95

Snow
Shed

No Name

96

To:
Silverton &
Durango

80. Portland Mine Amphitheater
81. Practice Rock
82. French Slabs
83. Bear Creek Falls
84. Sun Splash
85. Solar Circus
86. Horsetail Falls
87. Wild Horses
88. Mixed Emotions
89. Kennedy's Gully
90. Blue Condition
91. Abraxas
92. Gravity's Rainbow
93. Over The Rainbow
94. More Thin Slabs
95. Big Bad Avi Chutes
96. Snow Shed Walls

South of Ouray, upriver from the Ice Park, there are several worthy ice climbs. Snowy road conditions can make the driving in this area treacherous. Chains and/or 4-wheel drive is required by law much of the winter. Avalanche danger can be extreme.

❏ 80. Portland Mine Amphitheater
Grade: WI4 to 5
Height: 350'+
Approach: 30+ minutes
Land Status: National Forest
Avalanche Danger: Moderate to high
Best Season: Mid winter
Special Gear: V-Thread, headlamp

Several icefalls form in this area. The main line forms just left of center in the main cirque. Descent: Rappel the route. Several other routes can be climbed in this area (WI3 to 4).

❏ 81. Practice Rock, WI3 to 4, a verglass-covered slab that is usually top-roped.

❏ 82. French Slabs, WI2 to 3, often thin.

BEAR CREEK

This area is about 2.5 miles south of Ouray on HWY 550. Park in pullout on right.

❏ 83. Bear Creek Falls
Grade: WI5
Height: 150'
Approach: 5 minutes
Land Status: National Forest
Avalanche Danger: Moderate to high
Best Season: Early season

Below the bridge you will often find wet and rotten ice to climb, usually in shape sometime in early season.

❏ 84. Sun Splash (topo p. 63)
Grade: WI5
Height: 500'+
Approach: 30 minutes
Land Status: National Forest
Avalanche Danger: Moderate to high
Best Season: Early through mid winter
Special Gear: V-Thread, headlamp, rock gear, Jumars optional

Takes the obvious gully/corner system. Conditions can be thin and mixed. Normally climbed in 5 pitches. Approach by scrambling up the rock ridge above the parking area (just south of the bridge). Walk along the terrace and rappel to the base of the climbs. You can leave a tied off rope to Jumar out.

85. Solar Circus

Grade: WI4
Height: 300'
Approach: 30 minutes
Land Status: National Forest
Avalanche Danger: Moderate to extreme
Best Season: Mid to late winter
Special Gear: V-Thread, headlamp, rock gear, Jumars optional

A fine, moderate version of Gravity's Rainbow, climbed in two to three pitches. Approach by scrambling up the rock ridge above the parking area (just south of the bridge). Walk along the terrace and rappel to the base of the climbs. You can leave a tied off rope to Jumar out.

86. Horsetail Falls

Grade: WI4 to 5
Height: 500'
Approach: 15 to 20 minutes
Land Status: National Forest
Avalanche Danger: Moderate to high
Best Season: Early through mid winter
Special Gear: V-Thread, headlamp

This is a classic ice climb for sure. Walk down the steep hillside just south of the bridge and cross the frozen river. One of the best climbs on Red Mountain Pass. Descent Walk off and down left.

87. Wild Horses

Grade: WI3 to 4
Height: 700'
Approach: 15 to 20 minutes
Land Status: National Forest
Avalanche Danger: Moderate to high
Best Season: Early season
Special Gear: V-Thread, headlamp

This route is a fun early season route. It is covered with snow most of the winter.

HORSETAIL FALLS

BEAR CREEK

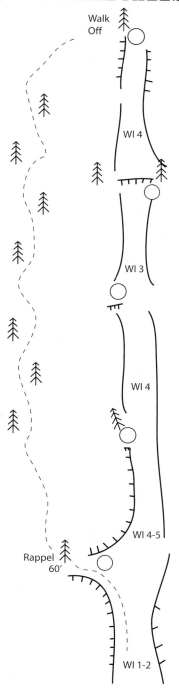

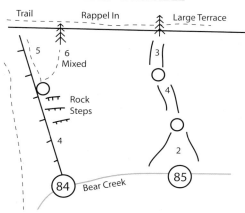

❏ 88. Mixed Emotions
Grade: WI5 to 6
Height: 150'
Approach: 10 minutes
Land Status: National Forest
Avalanche Danger: Moderate to high
Best Season: Mid to late winter
Special Gear: Rock gear

❏ 89. Kennedy's Gully
Grade: WI5
Height: 1200'
Approach: 10 minutes
Land Status: National Forest
Avalanche Danger: Moderate to high
Best Season: Early through mid winter
Special Gear: V-Thread, headlamp

Most parties do the first two steeper pitches and rappel off. Pitch 1 is WI3, Pitch 2 can be WI5. The upper gully is WI3 to 4 and mixed—rock gear is a must. Descent: Rappel the route.

❏ 90. Blue Condition
Grade: WI5
Height: 200'
Approach: 10 minutes
Land Status: National Forest
Avalanche Danger: Moderate to high
Best Season: Early through mid winter

R
E
D

M
T

P
A
S
S

GRAVITY'S RAINBOW AREA

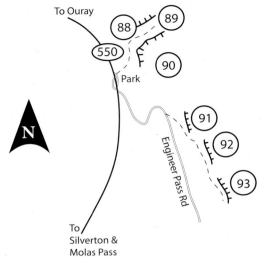

88. Mixed Emotions
89. Kennedy's Gully
90. Blue Condition
91 Abraxas
92. Gravity's Rainbow
93. Over The Rainbow

R
E
D

M
T

P
A
S
S

❑ 91. Abraxas
Grade: WI5 to 6
Height: 300'
Approach: 10 minutes
Land Status: National Forest
Avalanche Danger: moderate to high
Best Season: Early through mid winter
Special Gear: V-Thread, headlamp, rock gear

Rarely in condition, this route involves three pitches of thin, mixed climbing. Descen
Rappel the route.

❑ 92. Gravity's Rainbow
Grade: WI5
Height: 500'
Approach: 10 minutes
Land Status: National Forest
Avalanche Danger: Low to moderate
Best Season: Early through mid winter
Special Gear: V-Thread, headlamp, rock gear

Pitch 1: Often thin, poorly protected, and can be mixed
Pitch 2: Thicker ice than first pitch
Pitch 3: Short pitch to the base of the headwall
Pitch 4: Long pitch up steep, thick ice

Descent: There is a rappel route to the left of the climb; many fixed rock anchors to rap from. An early ascent is recommended as the sun can make climbing wet and "interesting."

☐ 93. Over The Rainbow
Grade: WI4 to 5
Height: 100 to 300'
Approach: 10 minutes
Land Status: National Forest
Avalanche Danger: Moderate to high
Best Season: Early through mid winter

Three 1 to 2 pitch climbs of thick ice. Descent: Rappel or walk off (avalanche danger can be high).

☐ **94. More Thin Slabs**, WI 3 to 5, 100-200'. Several thin slab routes can form here (not common).

☐ **95. Big Bad Avi Chutes**, WI3. Several obvious gullies that are fun in early season when avalanche conditions are low—avoid in mid winter and after large storms. Special gear: V-Thread and rock gear.

☐ **96. Snow Shed Walls**, WI5, 600'. Many variations.

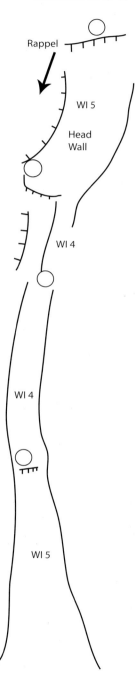

GRAVITY'S RAINBOW

Rappel

WI 5

Head Wall

WI 4

WI 4

WI 5

Gravity's Rainbow / © Doug Berry / Telluride Stock

SILVERTON

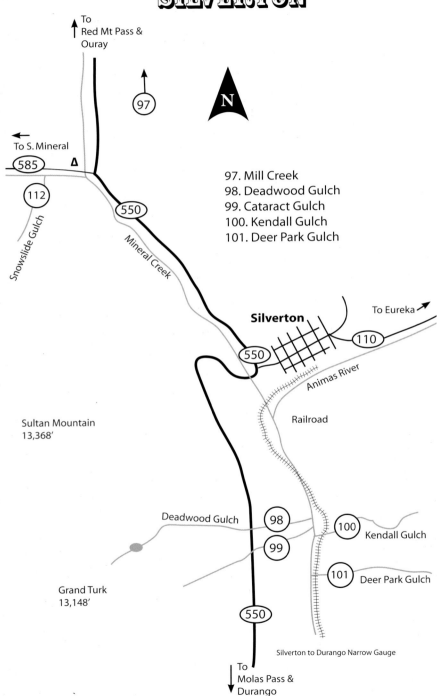

To
Red Mt Pass &
Ouray

(97)

N

To S. Mineral
(585)   Δ

(112)

Snowslide Gulch

(550)

Mineral Creek

97. Mill Creek
98. Deadwood Gulch
99. Cataract Gulch
100. Kendall Gulch
101. Deer Park Gulch

To Eureka

Silverton

(550)

(110)

Animas River

SILVERTON

Sultan Mountain
13,368'

Railroad

Deadwood Gulch

(98)

(100)

Kendall Gulch

(99)

(101)

Deer Park Gulch

Grand Turk
13,148'

(550)

Silverton to Durango Narrow Gauge

To
Molas Pass &
Durango

Another historic old mining town, Silverton tends to be fairly quite in the winter. That said, the new ski area that accesses a lot of extreme ski terrain has livened things up a bit. If you happen to be hauling your skis around with you, a day of skiing above Silverton is worth the price. For more information: www.silvertonmountain.com. At the moment, there are 13 establishments, ranging from cafes and restaurants to breweries and saloons, that serve food. For restocking food supplies, there is a market on the left just as you enter town from HWY 550. Silverton lacks the diversity of ice found around Telluride, but what *is* found in this area is very good. This area is know also for the two outlying areas—South Mineral Creek and Eureka. There can be good drivable access to many long routes early in the season. Many of the routes in this area are considered alpine climbs, therefore you should bring a headlamp, rock gear, and dress for it.

❏ 97. Mill Creek (not on map)
Grade: WI3
Height: 1000'
Approach: 20 minutes
Land Status: National Forest
Avalanche Danger: Moderate to high
Best Season: Early through mid winter
Special Gear:V-Thread, headlamp, rock gear
From Silverton: Look for Mill Creek just before coming into Chattanooga in the middle of the very large bend in the road.

❏ 98. Deadwood Gulch
Grade: WI3
Height: 100'+
Approach: 15 minutes
Land Status: National Forest
Avalanche Danger: Moderate to high
Best Season: Early season
Special Gear:V-Thread, headlamp

Park at the visitors center on the right as you enter town, and decidedly trespass along the narrow gauge railroad tracks.

❏ 99. Cataract Gulch
Grade: WI3
Height: 100'+
Approach: 15 minutes
Land Status: National Forest
Avalanche Danger: Moderate to high
Best Season: Early season
Special Gear:V-Thread, headlamp, rock gear

Park at the visitors center on the right as you enter town, and decidedly trespass along the narrow gauge railroad tracks. This route is not in climbable conditions often.

100. Kendall Gulch

Grade: WI4-
Height: 450'+
Approach: 45 minutes
Land Status: National Forest
Avalanche Danger: Moderate to high
Best Season: Early season
Special Gear: V-Thread, headlamp, rock gear

Park at the visitors center on the right as you enter town, and decidedly trespass along the narrow gauge railroad tracks. Begin climbing by the old water tank. The crux is at the top. Descent: Walk off left.

101. Dear Park Gulch

Grade: WI4
Height: 300'
Approach: 45 minutes
Land Status: National Forest
Avalanche Danger: Moderate to high
Best Season: Early season
Special Gear: V-Thread, headlamp, rock gear

Park at the visitors center on the right as you enter town, and decidedly trespass along the narrow gauge railroad tracks. This route does not form as consistently as Kendall Gulch.

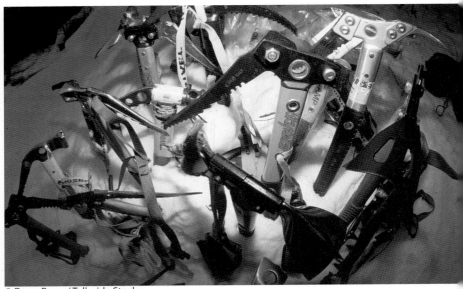

© Doug Berry / Telluride Stock

SOUTH MINERAL CREEK

To
Red Mt Pass &
Ouray

S. Mineral Creek

Peak
12,579'

Bear
Mountain

Porcupine Creek

N

102. Small Cascade
103. The Smear
104. Porcupine Creek
105. Campground Couloir
106. Snowblind
107. Direct North Face

108. Cataract Creek
109. Sundance
110. WI4 Steps
111. WI3 to 4 Steps Up High
112. Snow Slide

Several excellent long climbs are found in this valley. Most are narrow gullies and ice-choked chimneys. Unfortunately, many of these climbs are in very large avalanche paths in mid winter. They should only be climbed in early season, before the snow flies, or in a dry season when avalanche danger is lower than normal. Until the snows close the road—hint—it is possible to drive very near to the climbs. If the road is closed you must hike or ski in 5 miles. In addition, there is a campground near the climbs.

The best climbs in the area are on Peak 12,579. When done in their entirety, they are over 1000' high, though many parties choose to descend after climbing the initial harder ice sections. There are many more climbs in the area not covered in this book. Only the most interesting or commonly forming routes are included.

❏ 102. Small Cascade
Grade: WI3 to 4
Height: 40'
Approach: 20 minutes
Land Status: National Forest
Avalanche Danger: Moderate to extreme
Best Season: Early season or a very dry mid season
Special Gear: V-Thread, headlamp, rock gear

103. The Smear
Grade: WI2 to 3
Height: 300'
Approach: 20 minutes
Land Status: National Forest
Avalanche Danger: Moderate to extreme
Best Season: Early season or a very dry mid season
Special Gear: V-Thread, headlamp, rock gear

An obvious moderate slab.

104. Porcupine Creek
Grade: WI3 to 4
Height: 400'+
Approach: 45 minutes
Land Status: National Forest
Avalanche Danger: Moderate to extreme
Best Season: Early season or a very dry mid season
Special Gear: V-Thread, headlamp

A long, mostly moderate, streambed climb.

105. Campground Couloir
Grade: WI4
Height: 1000'
Approach: 20 minutes
Land Status: National Forest
Avalanche Danger: Moderate to extreme
Best Season: Early season or a very dry mid season
Special Gear: V-Thread, headlamp, rock gear

This is a striking blue strand of ice. Most parties do the first three pitches only (WI4). It is possible to continue for quite a ways up on WI2 to 3 ice. Descend: rappel route or walk down steep hillside to the right. It is possible to start this route to the right and left of the center.

106. Snowblind
Grade: WI5-
Height: 1000'
Approach: 10 to 15 minutes
Land Status: National Forest
Avalanche Danger: Moderate to extreme
Best Season: Early season or a very dry mid season
Special Gear: V-Thread, headlamp, rock gear

This is the obvious ice-filled chimney. It is longer than it looks. Five pitches lead to the top of the main difficulties. Optional: WI2 to 3 ice above steeper sections. Descent: walk down steep hillside to the left or rappel the route.

❏ 107. Direct North Face

Grade: WI5 to 6
Height: 1500'
Approach: 20 minutes
Land Status: National Forest
Avalanche Danger: Moderate to extreme
Best Season: Early season or a very dry mid season
Special Gear: V-Thread, headlamp, rock gear

A long and varied climb: Start up thin slabs and ramps leading to steep pencils of ice. Descent to the left. An excellent outing.

❏ 108. Cataract Creek

Grade: WI3 to 4
Height: 1000'+
Approach: 15 minutes
Land Status: National Forest
Avalanche Danger: Moderate to extreme
Best Season: Early season or a very dry mid season
Special Gear: V-Thread, headlamp, rock gear

A fun streambed. Walk off left.

❏ 109. Sundance

Grade: WI4 to 5
Height: 180'
Approach: 15 - 20 minutes
Land Status: National Forest
Avalanche Danger: Moderate to extreme
Best Season: Early season or a very dry mid season
Special Gear: V-Thread, headlamp, rock gear

There are two options for climbing this route. Right WI4 and left WI5. Walk off right.

Three avalanche gullies that are icy in early season.

❏ 110. WI4 steps

❏ 111. WI3 to 4 steps up high

❏ 112. Snowslide, WI2 to 3 narrow strand of ice

EUREKA

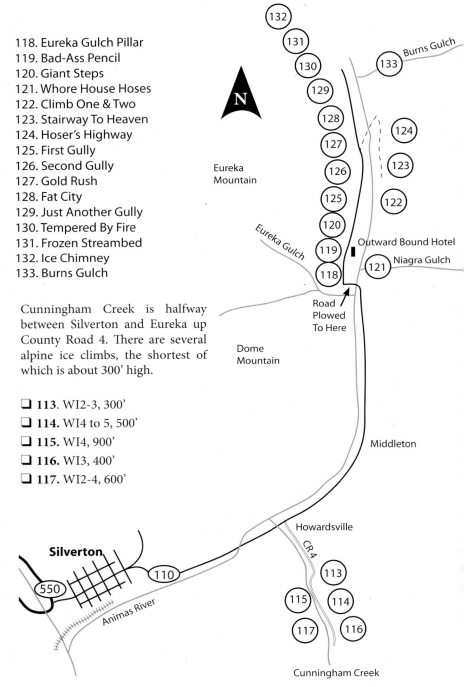

118. Eureka Gulch Pillar
119. Bad-Ass Pencil
120. Giant Steps
121. Whore House Hoses
122. Climb One & Two
123. Stairway To Heaven
124. Hoser's Highway
125. First Gully
126. Second Gully
127. Gold Rush
128. Fat City
129. Just Another Gully
130. Tempered By Fire
131. Frozen Streambed
132. Ice Chimney
133. Burns Gulch

Cunningham Creek is halfway between Silverton and Eureka up County Road 4. There are several alpine ice climbs, the shortest of which is about 300' high.

❏ **113**. WI2-3, 300'
❏ **114**. WI4 to 5, 500'
❏ **115**. WI4, 900'
❏ **116**. WI3, 400'
❏ **117**. WI2-4, 600'

SILVERTON

N

Burns Gulch

Eureka Mountain

Eureka Gulch

Outward Bound Hotel

Niagra Gulch

Road Plowed To Here

Dome Mountain

Middleton

Howardsville

CR 4

Silverton

550

110

Animas River

Cunningham Creek

Eureka is a veritable gold mine of ice climbs, ice filled chimneys and gullies are the norm; many are long—most just short of 1000'. Until the heavy snows close the road, it is possible to drive near to the climbs. Avalanche danger can be extreme in mid-winter or after a heavy snow fall. Early season is best for climbing these routes. Climbs north of the Outward Bound Hotel are in National Forest Lands. However, south of this point is mostly private land—no access problems have been reported. If you encounter an area that is posted please respect the land owners right and do not trespass. The character of the many climbs on the east flank of Peak 12634 varies considerably from year to year. This guide records climbs that can be expected to form up early in the season. A lot of ice forms in this area—many variations exist to most climbs. With careful route finding, most climbs can be descended by scrambling down to one side or the other. However, most parties elect to rappel the route using V-Threads and other make shift anchors.

☐ 118. Eureka Gulch Pillar
Grade: WI5
Height: 60'
Approach: 10 minutes
Land Status: Private, but seems to not be a problem
Avalanche Danger: Moderate to extreme
Best Season: Early season or a dry mid season
Special Gear: V-Thread, headlamp, rock gear

☐ 119. Bad-Ass Pencil
Grade: WI5 to 6
Height: 80'+
Approach: 5 minutes
Land Status: Private, but seems to not be a problem
Avalanche Danger: Moderate to extreme
Best Season: Early season or a dry mid season
Special Gear: V-Thread, headlamp, rock gear

☐ 120. Giant Steps
Grade: WI5
Height: 250'+
Approach: 30 minutes
Land Status: Private, but seems to not be a problem
Avalanche Danger: Moderate to extreme
Best Season: Early season or a dry mid season
Special Gear: V-Thread, headlamp, rock gear

High up on the hillside, climb two pitches—rappel off or scramble down steep slopes.

121. Whore House Hoses

Grade: WI5
Height: 600'+
Approach: 25 minutes
Land Status: Private, but seems to not be a problem
Avalanche Danger: Moderate to extreme
Best Season: Early season or a dry mid season
Special Gear: V-Thread, headlamp, rock gear

This is a big deep chimney. This climb is normally climbed in three pitches. There are
optional pitches up higher – at the top the right variation is harder (WI4+). There are
fixed anchors all the way. Rappel the climb.

122. Climb One and Two (a.k.a. Highway To Hell & Road To Nowhere)

Grade: WI4+ (discontinuous)
Height: 800'
Approach: 30 minutes
Land Status: National Forest
Avalanche Danger: Moderate to extreme
Best Season: Early season or a dry mid season
Special Gear: V-Thread, headlamp, rock gear

123. Stairway To Heaven

Grade: WI4
Height: 900'
Approach: 25 minutes
Land Status: National Forest
Avalanche Danger: Moderate to extreme
Best Season: Early season or a dry mid season
Special Gear: V-Thread, headlamp, rock gear

This is a very popular route—often you will be sharing it with other parties or resign
to coming back another day (having people climbing ice way above you is a bad idea).
This route is the obvious staircase. Descent: walk off left, rappel from trees, or rappel
the route with V-Threads.

124. Hoser's Highway

Grade: WI5+ (discontinuous)
Height: 1000'
Approach: 10 to 15 minutes
Land Status: National Forest
Avalanche Danger: Moderate to extreme
Best Season: Early season or a dry mid season
Special Gear: V-Thread, headlamp, rock gear

Two parallel gullies: Left: Lots of WI1 to 3 to a pillar (curx) midway up. Right: climbs thin slabs to start, crux is up high. Descent: a long and tedious walk off to the left.

❏ 125. First Gully
Grade: WI4
Height: 800'
Approach: 10 minutes
Land Status: National Forest
Avalanche Danger: Moderate to extreme
Best Season: Early season or a dry mid season
Special Gear: V-Thread, headlamp, rock gear

Rappel down the second gully.

❏ 126. Second Gully
Grade: WI4
Height: 800'
Approach: 5 minutes
Land Status: National Forest
Avalanche Danger: Moderate to extreme
Best Season: Early season or a dry mid season
Special Gear: V-Thread, headlamp, rock gear

The standard rappel route. First & Second Gullies are fun easy climbs for the area. They can be thin and mixed in places. Many variations exist that offer more challenging climbing. There are several WI5 pitches that form to the right of the main line of Second Gully.

❏ 127. Gold Rush
Grade: WI4 to 5
Height: 500'
Approach: 10 minutes
Land Status: National Forest
Avalanche Danger: Moderate to extreme
Best Season: Early season or a dry mid season
Special Gear: V-Thread, headlamp, rock gear

Climb the ramp up the left wall of the big left facing corner.

❏ 128. Three Fine Climbs (a.k.a. Fat City Area)
Grade WI3 to 5
Height: 800'
Approach:
Land Status: National Forest
Avalanche Danger: Moderate to extreme
Best Season: Early season or a dry mid season
Special Gear: V-Thread, headlamp, rock gear

Left: Slab, WI3, one pitch
Middle: Steeper slabs with a mixed exit, WI4
Right: Fat City, WI5. A thick pillar that climbs two pitches to easier climbing. Most parties only climb the WI5 and rappel off.

❏ 129. Just Another Gully
Grade: WI3
Height: 800'
Approach: 10 mminutes
Land Status: National Forest
Avalanche Danger: Moderate to extreme
Best Season: Early season or a dry mid season
Special Gear: V-Thread, headlamp, rock gear

Another long moderate with a WI5 variation at the top to the right.

❏ 130. Tempered By Fire
Grade: WI4+
Height: 180'+
Approach: 5 minutes
Land Status: National Forest
Avalanche Danger: Moderate to extreme
Best Season: Early season or a dry mid season
Special Gear: V-Thread, headlamp, rock gear

Climb ice-filled chimney to a steep pillar. Descent: Walk off right.

❏ 131. Yet Another Frozen Streambed
Grade: WI3
Height: 200'+ (additional climbing to be considered depending on conditions)
Approach: 15+ minutes
Land Status: National Forest
Avalanche Danger: Moderate to extreme
Best Season: Early season or a dry mid season
Special Gear: V-Thread, headlamp, rock gear

132. Yet Another Iced Chimney
Grade: WI4+
Height: 165'
Approach: 5 minutes
Land Status: National Forest
Avalanche Danger: Moderate to extreme
Best Season: Early season or a dry mid season
Special Gear: V-Thread, headlamp, rock gear

Descent: Walk off left

133. Burns Gulch
Grade: WI4
Height: 50'
Approach: 30 mminutes
Land Status: National Forest
Avalanche Danger: Moderate to extreme
Best Season: Early season or a dry mid season
Special Gear: V-Thread, headlamp, rock gear

A short, steep, thick step.

© Doug Berry / Telluride Stock

To Ouray

Silverton

550

Molas Creek

W. Lime Creek

Park

138

139

137

E. Lime Cr

Cascade Creek

142

141

Park

136

140

Purgatory
Ski Area

550

Old
Lime Creek Rd

135

17.5 miles
to Durango

134

Animas River

Note: Old Lime Creek Rd
is not plowed in winter,
therefore, skis make the
approach much faster.

Best to start your ski from the
north and ski downhill, 12 miles
total, back to HWY 550.

Hermosa

**D
U
R
A
N
G
O**

Durango
Area

550

550

Durango

134. Highway Robbery
135. Seven Year Itch
136. Cascade Creek
137. Deer Creek
138. Lime Creek Curtain
139. Molas Creek
140. Twilight Peak
141. Carter Creek
142. Three Lakes Creek

N

134. Highway Robbery
Grade: WI3
Height: 100'
Approach: 20 minutes
Land Status: National Forest, crosses private land, access has not been an issue
Avalanche Danger: Low to moderate
Best Season: Mid to late winter

Drive about 2.5 miles north of Hermosa on HWY 550. Park at the US Forest Service sign and hike up a short ways on the west side of the valley to the base of the route. Descent: Rappel from trees.

135. Seven Year Itch
Grade: WI5-
Height: 300'
Approach: 20 minutes
Land Status: National Forest, crosses private land, access has not been an issue
Avalanche Danger: Low to moderate
Best Season: Mid to late winter

Climb forms rarely. Two short pitches lead to one long pitch. Descent: Rappel from trees.

136. Cascade Creek
Grade: WI2 to 5
Height: 60'+/- depends on climb
Approach: 5- minutes
Land Status: National Forest
Avalanche Danger: Low to moderate
Best Season: Mid to late winter

Lots to do and a short walk around makes this is an excellent area to top-rope ice routes. A mile north of Durango Mountain Resort, park at the large pull-out where the old Lime Creek Road—County Rd 1—intersects HWY 550. Rappel in or climb down below the cattle guard. Descent: Rappel from trees.

"I have heard it said that it takes more courage to retreat than to advance. I cannot share these sentiments!"
— René Desmaison

❏ 137. Deer Creek
Grade: WI5
Height: 80'
Approach: 15 minutes
Land Status: National Forest
Avalanche Danger: Low to moderate
Best Season: All winter
Descent: Rappel from trees

❏ 138. Lime Creek Curtain
Grade: WI4 to 5
Height: 300'
Approach: 5 minutes
Land Status: National Forest
Avalanche Danger: Low to moderate
Best Season: Mid to late winter

Climb three steep sections of water ice—crux is at the top. Located about three miles south of Molas Pass. Descent: Rappel from trees.

❏ 139. Molas Creek
Grade: WI3 to 4
Height: 70'
Approach: 20+ minutes
Land Status: National Forest
Avalanche Danger: Low
Best Season: Early season
Special Gear: Headlamp, skis can be of some use here depending on snow conditions
Descent: Walk off

OLD LIME CREEK ROAD AREA

These climbs are best accessed by parking at the pullout by the Old Lime Creek Road's north entrance. Because the slope of the old road is slightly downhill, you can ski the six miles in fairly quickly.

❏ 140. Twilight Peak
Grade: WI4 to 5
Height: 100'
Approach: 1.5 hours
Land Status: National Forest
Avalanche Danger: Moderate to extreme
Best Season: Early season
Special Gear: V-Thread, headlamp, rock gear
Descent: Rappel from trees

❏ 141. Carter Creek
Grade: WI4 to 5
Height: 300'+
Approach: 1.5 hours
Land Status: National Forest
Avalanche Danger: Moderate to extreme
Best Season: Early season
Special Gear: V-Thread, headlamp, rock gear

Follow the streambed up high to the WI4 to 5 pitch of ice. Descent: Rappel from trees.

❏ 142. Three Lakes Creek
Grade: WI3 to 4
Height: 100'
Approach: 1.5 hours
Land Status: National Forest
Avalanche Danger: Moderate to extreme
Best Season: Early season
Special Gear: V-Thread, headlamp, rock gear

Another long streambed climb with a headwall up high. Descent: Rappel from trees.

DURANGO

N

To
Molas Pass &
Silverton

550

Hermosa

Animas River

147 Freed
Canyon

203   252

146 Haflin   145
Canyon

143. East Animas Ice Climb
144. Woodlard Canyon
145. Haflin Canyon Falls upper
146. Haflin Canyon Falls Lower
147. Freed Canyon Falls

144 Woodard
Canyon

250

143 East
Animas

Durango

32nd St

DURANGO

Florida Raod

To
Cortez   160

550

To
Wolf Creek Pass (160)

82

Durango is a nice little city on the southern edge of the San Juan Mountains. Supermarkets, cheap hotels, climbing shops, stoplights, and other city-kind-of-things are found in Durango. There are several areas to find ice, but it is a bit on the short side. Most routes in this area are under 100' with a few exceptions. There are several ice climbs between Silverton and Durango which are covered in the Durango North section. Animas City Mountain, has good bouldering and top-roping.

❏ 143. East Animas Ice Climb
Grade: WI5
Height: 60'
Approach: 5 minutes
Land Status: National Forest
Avalanche Danger: Low to moderate
Best Season: Mid winter
Descent: Rappel off trees

❏ 144. Woodard Canyon
Grade: WI4 to 5
Height: 120'
Approach: 15- minutes
Land Status: National Forest
Avalanche Danger: Low to moderate
Best Season: Mid winter

Climb a pillar to a gully. Descent: Rappel off trees.

❏ 145. Haflin Canyon Upper Falls
Grade: WI5
Height: 120'
Approach: 1 hour+ (up to 1.5 hours)
Land Status: National Forest
Avalanche Danger: Low to moderate
Best Season: Mid winter

To reach the upper falls expect a 2.5 mile hike. Take the left fork in the trail. This route does not come into climbing shape often. Descent: Rappel off trees.

❏ 146. Haflin Canyon Lower Falls
Grade: WI5
Height: 50'+
Approach: 15 minutes
Land Status: National Forest
Avalanche Danger: Low to moderate
Best Season: Mid winter
Descent: Rappel off trees

❏ 147. Freed Canyon Falls
Grade: WI5
Height: 75'
Approach: 5 minutes
Land Status: Private, but OK
Avalanche Danger: Low to moderate
Best Season: Mid winter

Park 1.5 miles past the timberland intersection. Be sure to park out of the way of traffic and the snowplows path. You will cross private land, but there has not been an issue to date. Descent: Rappel off trees.

Avalanche ripping down Mt Hunter, Alaska / © Damon Johnston

LAKE CITY

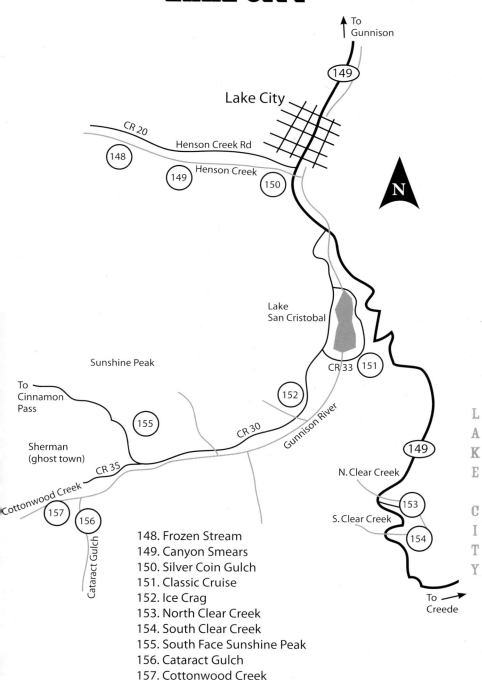

To Gunnison

149

Lake City

CR 20

Henson Creek Rd

148

149   Henson Creek

150

N

Lake
San Cristobal

Sunshine Peak

CR 33   151

To
Cinnamon
Pass

152

155

CR 30

Gunnison River

Sherman
(ghost town)

CR 35

149

Cottonwood Creek

N. Clear Creek

157   156

S. Clear Creek

153

Cataract Gulch

154

L
A
K
E

C
I
T
Y

To
Creede

148. Frozen Stream
149. Canyon Smears
150. Silver Coin Gulch
151. Classic Cruise
152. Ice Crag
153. North Clear Creek
154. South Clear Creek
155. South Face Sunshine Peak
156. Cataract Gulch
157. Cottonwood Creek

Things have changed a bit since the last guide book was published, and Lake City is no exception. Today, there are two handfuls of restaurants (Poker Alice is a favorite for stone-baked pizza) including an internet cafe. There is an abundance of lodging but only about a quarter of them are open in the winter. There are also options for camping. If circumstances allow, take in a movie at the Mountaineer Movie Theatre. Lake City's official website is helpful: www.lakecity.com. Further information about ice climbing in and near Lake City can be found at www.lakecitywinter.com/iceclimbing.html.

HENSON CREEK AREA

This area is located about two to four miles outside of Lake City to the east.

❑ **148. Frozen Stream** (a.k.a. Wet Muppet)
Grade: WI4
Height: 200'
Approach: 15 minutes
Land Status: National Forest (watch for private land in this area)
Avalanche Danger: Low
Best Season: Mid winter

Located four miles from town on the south side of the road (just past the mining community). Descent: Rappel from trees.

❑ **149. Canyon Smears** (a.k.a. Henson Creek)
Grade: WI3 to 4
Height: 50 to 100'+
Approach: 5 minutes
Land Status: National Forest (watch for private land in this area)
Avalanche Danger: Low
Best Season: Mid winter

Occasionally, a few short climbs form up in the canyon. This area is 2 miles out of town on the south side of the road. Good top-roping area. Descent: Rappel from trees.

❑ **150. Silver Coin Gulch**
Grade: WI4
Height: 80'
Approach: 5 minutes
Land Status: National Forest (watch for private land in this area)
Avalanche Danger: Low
Best Season: Mid winter

LAKE SAN CRISTOBAL

❏ **151. Classic Cruise**
Grade: WI4
Height: 250'
Approach: 15 minutes
Land Status: National Forest
Avalanche Danger: Low
Best Season: Mid winter

❏ **152. Crag Ice**, WI4+. Located 7 miles from town and up the hill on the rock buttress to the northeast.

CLEAR CREEK

This area is found about 21 miles outside of Lake City as your drive towards Creede.

❏ **153. North Clear Creek Falls**
Grade: WI3 to 5
Height: 90'
Approach: 5 minutes
Land Status: National Forest
Avalanche Danger: None
Best Season: Mid winter

Drive or ski 1/2 mile to the picnic area atop the falls. Rappel in.

❏ **154. South Clear Creek Falls**
Grade: WI4 to 5
Height: 70'
Approach: 5 minutes
Land Status: National Forest
Avalanche Danger: None
Best Season: Mid winter

Park at the old campground and follow a nice trail to the base of the falls.

SHERMAN - COTTONWOOD CREEK

❏ **155. South Face Of Sunshine Peak**
Grade: WI2 to 5
Height: 200 to 700'
Approach: 20 minutes
Land Status: National Forest
Avalanche Danger: Moderate to extreme
Best Season: Mid winter

The descent can be a challenge; bring extra slings, a few pins, and use trees fro rappel. Bring rock gear. This route faces south so conditions can change quickly.

❏ **156. Cataract Gulch,** WI4 to 5, 150' and other climbs.

❏ **157. Cottonwood Creek** has many ice routes making the hike in (1.5 to 2.5 miles) worth the trip. There are two multi-pitch WI5's that are 300' to 500' high.

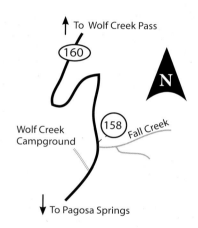

WOLF CREEK PASS

There are several ice climbs in this area. Only one route is represented in this guide.

❏ **158. Treasure Falls**
Grade: WI4 to 5
Height: 130'
Approach: 15 minutes
Land Status: National Forest
Avalanche Danger: Moderate to high
Best Season: Early to mid winter
Special Gear: Headlamp

This is a long-time, year-round, tourist attraction with a parking area and signs pointing out Treasure Falls to everyone that drives by. It is located about eight miles west of the top of the pass. Descent: Rappel from trees.

BLUE MESA

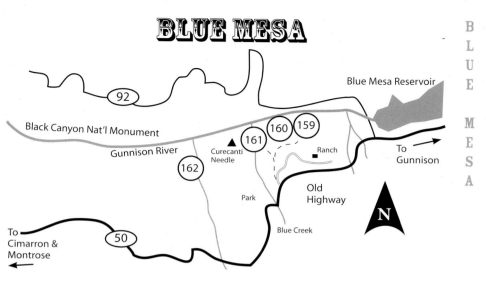

The approaches are often the crux of climbing these routes. You can see many of these climbs well from Pioneer Point on HWY 92. Do not park near the ranch (private property). The approach may cross private land—keep your activity on the down low.

❏ **159. Blue Mesa Smear**, WI4 to 5, 140'. One hour approach, best in mid winter. Descent: Rappel the route or hike up to mesa.

❏ **160. Blue Balls**, WI3 to 4, 300'. One hour approach, best in mid winter. Descent: Rrappel the route or hike up to mesa.

❏ **161. Blue Creek**, WI4, 300'. A 2 pitch gully climb. Left: WI3+, slightly shorter.

❏ **162. Fat Steam**, WI3+, 280'+. One hour approach, best in mid winter, Descent: Rappel the route.

DUNTON

This area is found between Rico and Dolores to the west.

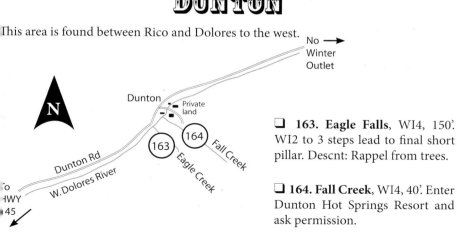

❏ **163. Eagle Falls**, WI4, 150'. WI2 to 3 steps lead to final short pillar. Descnt: Rappel from trees.

❏ **164. Fall Creek**, WI4, 40'. Enter Dunton Hot Springs Resort and ask permission.

RECOMMENDED ROUTES

CHIMNEYS, GULLYS & STREAMBEDS
❑ Bird Brain Boulevard - Ouray - p. 56
❑ Direct N. Face, Peak 12579 - S. Mineral Cr. - p. 71
❑ Ames Ice Hose - Ames - p. 38
❑ Snowblind, S. Mineral Cr. - p. 70
❑ Whore House Hoses - Eureka - p. 74
❑ Gravity's Rainbow - Red Mt. Pass - P. 64
❑ Stairway To Heaven - Eureka - p. 74
❑ Cracked Canyon Ice Fall - Ophir - p. 41
❑ Campground Couloir - S. Mineral Cr. p. 70
❑ Out Of The Mainstream - Red. Mt Pass - p. 54
❑ Horsetail Falls - Ouray South - p. 62
❑ Second Gully - Eureka - p. 75

PRACTICE & TOP-ROPE AREAS
❑ Ouray Ice Park - Ouray - p. 48
❑ Ames Falls - Ames - p. 37
❑ Bear Creek - Telluride - p. 14
❑ Dexter Creek - Ouray - p. 45

WATERFALLS & PILLARS
❑ Bridal Veil Falls - Telluride East - p. 20
❑ Ingram Falls - Telluride East - p. 24
❑ Hoser's Highway - Eureka - p. 74
❑ Tangled Up in Blue - Ouray - p. 52
❑ Skyrocket Creek - Ouray N. - p. 46
❑ Cornet Falls - Telluride - p. 14
❑ The Fang - Telluride East - p. 18
❑ Silverpick - Telluride Down Valley - p. 34
❑ Royer Gulch - Telluride - p. 18
❑ Mill Creek Falls - Telluride - p. 16
❑ North Clear Creek - Lake City - p. 87
❑ Treasure Falls - Wolf Creek Pass - p. 88
❑ Freed - Durango - p. 84
❑ Jackass Falls - Telluride - p. 27
❑ Choppo's Chimney - Skylight - p. 59
❑ Skylight - Skylight - p. 59

CHARLIE'S FINAL NOTES

Final Notes, acknowledgements, apologies, excuses, and other bullshit......

This guide is the result of 14 years of iceclimbing in the San Juans. I ended up doing most of the routes in this guide — what a long, strang, weird, cold, wet, scary, and fun trip its been.

Sorry there's no record of first ascents in the book, but there's no way I could figure out who did what or when. You'd be surprised how many people told me they did the FA of certain routes.

Also I made up names for lots of climbs in the book. maybe the names arent the ones you use, OK so write your own guide.

I'd like to thank some of the people that helped me along the way, providing information, advice, inspiration, and mostly somebody to climb with:

Kevin Donald   Max Kendall
Sandy East   Axel Koch
Jeff Löwe   Kevin Cooney
Steve Johnson   Tom Polaski
James Hebert   Mark Wilford
Doug Scott   Greg Davis
Parker Newby   Layton Kor
John Burns   Alex Lowe
                      Doug Berry

I hope you enjoy these climbs as much as I did.

Charlie Fowler

Charlie Fowler's final notes from the second edition, 1996

mountain world media
GUIDEBOOKS & MOUNTAIN-RELATED LITERATURE

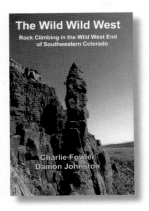

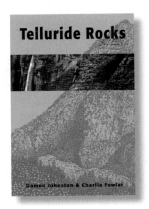

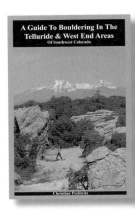

At a bookstore or gear shop near you!
(If not, please ask for them!)

MOUNTAIN STAR

A true story about a mountaineer that will teach kids how to draw a perfect star! Written by Ginny Fowler Hicks in memory of her brother, Charlie.

Online Consumer Orders
Chessler Books: www.chesslerbooks.com • 800-654-8502

Wholesale Orders
CO-UT-NM-AZ-WY-ID-MT
Bookswest: www.bookswest.com • 800-378-5995

ALL OTHERS
Alpenbooks: www.alpenbooks.com • 800-290-9898

Mountain World Media would like to hear about the guidebook you have been meaning to write, or even the one you've been meaning to update. Email us at damon@mountainworldmedia.com.